THE
HANDY
SPORTSMAN

THE HANDY SPORTSMAN

Loring D. Wilson

Photographs by the Author

STOEGER PUBLISHING COMPANY

Dedication

To Brenda—hunting companion, fishing buddy, and wife—through whose patience and understanding I have filled the house with the paraphernalia of the sportsman.

The chapters "Midge Vise," "Streamside Fly-Tying Kit," and "The Wilson Eel" originally appeared in slightly different form in *Flyfisher* magazine; "Custom Loading Bench" in *The Handloader;* and "Custom-Fitted Shotgun Case" in the *Publications of the American Rifle Association.*

I wish to express the sincerest gratitude to the staff of these magazines and especially to Ken Warner, Steve Raymond, and Dixie Goertemiller, whose kindness and encouragement have kept me at the typewriter.

Library of Congress Cataloging in Publication Data
Wilson, Loring D.
  The handy sportsman.
    1. Hunting—Implements and appliances.   2.   Fishing—
Implements and appliances.   3.   Handicraft.   I.   Title.
SK273.W5   799'.028   77-84337
ISBN 0-88317-041-8

Published by Stoeger Publishing Company
55 Ruta Court
South Hackensack, New Jersey 07606

First Stoeger quality paperback edition, August 1977

This Stoeger Sportsman's Library edition is published by
arrangement with Winchester Press.

Distributed to the book trade by Follett Publishing Company
and to the sporting goods trade by Stoeger Industries. In
Canada, distributed to the book trade and to the sporting
goods trade by Stoeger Trading Company.

Printed in the United States of America

Contents

I. Getting Started

1. The Handy Sportsman   3
2. Tools and Materials   6

II. For the Fisherman

3. Camera Case for Fishermen   19
4. Midge Vise   23
5. Streamside Fly-Tying Kit   29
6. The Wilson Eel   35
7. Emergency Fly Dressings   38
8. Wooden Tackle Box   41
9. Wooden Trout Net   55
10. Fly-Tying Desk   63
11. Portable Fly-Tying Bench   72
12. The Art of Making Wooden Plugs   76
13. Trolling Speed Indicator   92
14. Bug Cutter   95
15. Live Bag   100
16. Spinner Center   110
17. Rod Rack   117

III. For the Hunter

18. Custom Loading Bench 125
19. Custom-Fitted Shotgun Case 136
20. Game Carrier 142
21. Shotshell Carrier 147
22. Trapshooter's Box 152
23. Shotshell Trimmer 155
24. The Art of the Duck Decoy 162
25. Silhouette Dove Decoys 172
26. Squirrel Call 179
27. Turkey Call 183
28. Crow Call 188
29. Shooter's Bipod 190
30. Gun Cabinet 195

IV. Tips and Tricks 205

Appendix: Where to Find It 213

Index 215

1

GETTING STARTED

1

The Handy Sportsman

Spectator sports such as football, basketball, and baseball may well be the "national sports," but it is a well-known fact that hunters and fishermen spend far more money on their sports each year than all the spectators combined.

This is not difficult to understand. Real sports require precision equipment, equipment which does not come cheaply. Rifles and shotguns start at more than $100, and the price skyrockets into the thousands very easily. Fishing rods and reels can be had cheaply, but if the fisherman goes to a name brand, one which he can be certain will give many years of good—and I mean good—service, then we are talking about at least $30 for a rod, and between $30 and $50 (and up) for a decent reel—and of course, if the fisherman needs English split-bamboo fly rods and balanced reels, the Rolls Royces of fishing, then we are talking of thousands of dollars again.

But these are just the basic articles of equipment for each sport. Then come the accessories, some needed, some merely interesting additions. For the hunter, necessary additions include good boots, proper clothing for various climates, gun cases, telescopic sights if any long-range shooting is to be done, a gun sling, shell carriers, knife, and ammunition. And with the cost of the last item today, the hunter who does a great amount of shooting needs reloading equipment—press, dies, powder scale, powder measure, components, and various other necessary tools and materials.

For the fisherman, necessary equipment includes proper clothing, line, lures, tackle box, terminal tackle, in all likelihood a boat and motor, and if he ties his own flies, vise, scissors, hackle pliers, hooks, feathers, fur, and so on.

The nonessential, but handy, things to have are simply too numerous to mention. Certainly the sportsman can get along without them, but everyone who knows the sports of hunting and fishing knows the acquisitive nature of those sports, the experimenting with new things that goes on constantly. And this costs money.

Yet it doesn't have to cost so much as the major manufacturers of sporting goods would like you to think. With a few tools and some inexpensive materials, the handy sportsman can make for himself many things which will make his sport more enjoyable. This book presents step-by-step explanations of how to create these accessories, so that the sportsman with only moderate ability with tools can, in spare moments, build many things he would otherwise have to purchase. In some instances, he can make accessories which are not even available on the market.

Projects in this book range from the very simple to the moderately difficult; the materials cost ranges from about 25 cents to approximately $20. However, many of the projects utilize materials which would ordinarily be found in a home workshop, and so it is possible to reduce the cost of the project by using leftovers from other projects.

The following section on tools and materials presents some of the basics for the beginner. Special materials that are needed for each separate project are covered under the heading of that project. Although power tools ease the work to a great extent, every project in this volume can be built solely with hand tools.

Don't be afraid you won't be able to build any of the projects. Relax, enjoy the work, and it will turn out fine. If a project looks too complicated, save it for later. You will learn more as you go along, for the book is designed to introduce new techniques a little at a time; once you have mastered them on easy projects, the more complicated ones are that much easier. If you can cast a lure and fight a fish, or if you can handle a gun safely and shoot it accurately, you are handy enough to build any of the projects in this book, even if you have never built anything else before.

I chose the projects here for several reasons. As I have already said, they progress in difficulty with new skills taught. But more important, most sportsmen can use these things on the stream, in the field, or around the house to announce to all comers that they are sportsmen, continuing a long heritage, and damned proud of it. The projects are useful. You can completely outfit yourself for fishing if all you own is a rod, reel, and line—for I will show you how to build everything else that a fisherman normally needs: tackle box, landing net, plugs, spinners, flies, lures, and even a trolling-speed indicator to keep your lure at the right depth and speed. If all you own is a gun, I will show you how to outfit yourself with a custom-fitted gun case to protect your weapon, a carrier for shotshells and a carrier for game, decoys to bring the game within range, a squirrel call that really works, as well as a gun cabinet for the home to protect and display your long guns.

You may be surprised to find so much on handloading in a book of this sort. If you do not handload and you shoot a lot, you really should consider it, if not to work up more accurate loads, then at least to save money on shells and increase the amount you can shoot. There are two reasons for the number of handloading-gear projects: handloading is to shooters what fly-tying is to fly fishermen (not only a money-saving activity, but also a way to continue your sport well into the off-season); and, reloading gear is *expensive*. If you take up handloading, and build the projects in this book designed for the handloader, you can save a good third of the initial cost of pursuing this fascinating and rewarding extension of the shooting sports.

And in spite of the great proliferation of books on fly-tying, I have not left the fly-tier out either. I present him or her with a midge vise, a streamside fly-tying kit, a portable fly-tying bench, and several flies that are very effective and not often detailed in most fly-tying books.

Well, enough pep talk. Read the section on tools and materials next, and then browse through the rest of the book. No need to go straight through—in fact, it is more fun to skip around and make the things that interest you the most first. You can skim the chapters and adapt the project to how much time you have. But the most important thing, aside from very practical savings of money, is to have fun. Find a project that interests you, get the tools and materials laid out, and let's build something.

2
Tools and Materials

If you have read the introduction, you already know that all the projects in this book can be built with hand tools. This chapter will cover the hand tools necessary to complete all the projects in the book. Before you buy them all, however, look to see if you need them for the projects you want to build, as some have rather limited use. If not, then hold off buying them until you decide to make the projects that require them.

The section on hand tools is followed by a section on power tools, in case you want to add them to your tool collection. They aren't necessary, but they do make the work easier. Then follows a section on the basic materials you will need for the projects. Any materials of limited use will be covered under their particular project.

HAND TOOLS

Since practically all the projects in this book are made from wood, your primary tool will be a saw. You should have three varieties. There should be two standard carpenter's hand saws, a rip and a crosscut. The rip saw provides fast cutting with the grain of the wood; the crosscut saw, with more teeth to the inch, provides smooth cutting across the grain. A perfectly good saw can be had for as little as $5, and if you can afford only one, then get the crosscut saw, since it is more versatile. The other necessary saw is a coping saw, which consists of a handle, a deep frame, and a very thin blade. This is used for cutting curves and circles. Buy plenty of blades along with it, as they tend to break easily. The coping saw can be purchased for around $1.50; blades are a few cents apiece.

You also need a hammer. There are various hammers on the market. You need one with a 10-ounce head. Except for the gun cabinet, all of the projects are small, and do not require a heavier hammer. The gun cabinet is put together with screws, anyway. A hammer of this sort can be acquired for $2. Some hardware store clerks will say that the 10-ounce head is more expensive than the standard 16-ounce head because it is not standard. This is a basket of bullfeathers. Once the mold is set up, a 10-ounce head naturally costs less to make since it uses less steel. If anyone tries to boost the price on you, thank him politely, and go somewhere else.

The next item is a screwdriver. The choice here is more or less up to you. Some excellent screwdrivers run $1 or so apiece. These

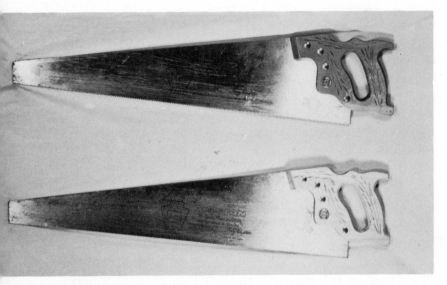

Rip saw (top) and crosscut saw.

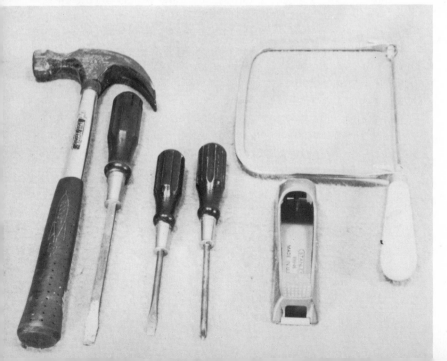

Hammer, screwdrivers, small plane, coping saw.

7

are hollow-ground, so that the blade fits the screw slot exactly. A ¼-inch blade and a ⅜-inch blade are all that are necessary.

However, sets of from six to ten screwdrivers in various sizes can be purchased in discount stores, and the cost of these sets is seldom more than $1.99. Actually, these inexpensive screwdrivers will do all you need them to do, and the various sizes do come in handy. Their disadvantages are that they are tapered, so that they may slip out of the screw slot and mar the head of the screw or the wood surrounding it, and if too much force is applied, the blades can break. But if you buy them solely for the projects in this book, get the set. They are cheap enough to replace if something does happen to them, and they perform well enough for our purposes.

A hand drill is the next tool needed. Hand drills come in two varieties, and both have their uses. The breast drill uses common twist bits from $1/16$ to ¼ inch in diameter. This drill can be had for about $4. The other variety, the brace and bit, will drill holes from ¼ inch to 1⅛ inches in diameter. Drill bits for the breast drill should be purchased as a set, as they have many, many uses, and a set for wood costs in the neighborhood of $2. The bits for the brace range from 70¢ to $2 apiece, and should be purchased as needed. However, before you buy either one of these drills, read my comments on the power drill in the next section.

A good pocket knife is also necessary for those projects which involve carving. I use a "whittlin'" knife with three blades. The overall length closed is about 3½ inches. Get a good one; a cheap knife is worse than none at all. Mine cost $5, and has given me excellent service for over ten years—both in the shop and in the field.

About the only other hand tools needed are pliers for the small amount of metalwork that has to be done. I like having two pairs on hand; one is of the "vise-grip" variety, the other of the electrician's long or needlenose type. The latter is excellent for making small bends in wire, as are used in a few projects. The former take care of all heavier bending operations, and when clamped to the workbench or table with a C-clamp, they serve as an excellent light-duty vise. Serviceable long-nose pliers can be had for as little as $1; the vise-grips run around $3 or $4, depending upon size.

You can also add clamps if you wish. They are an aid in gluing things together, and are relatively inexpensive. But large projects can be tied while glue is drying, and smaller projects can be tacked, so, although they are handy, they are not necessary. In the same line, a square is not absolutely essential. However, one can be obtained for $2, and on projects like the gun cabinet and the wooden tackle box, it

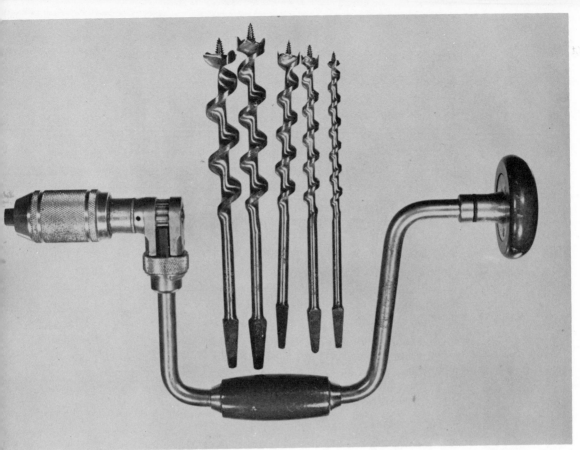

Hand drill and bits.

makes for a much better job. If you have the $2 extra, by all means get one.

That takes care of the necessary hand tools. With these tools you can, with care, build any of the projects in this book. However, before proceeding to the power tools, you may wish to add a few additional hand tools. In some cases they will make certain operations much easier, although greater care is required in their use than with some of the other hand tools.

The first of these additional tools is a chisel. The chisel is especially handy for making the squirrel call in the section for the hunter since, although the cuts can be made with a pocket knife, the wood is exceptionally hard, and a chisel will do a smoother job, more rapidly, with less danger to your hands. Chisels come in a wide variety of sizes and types, and differ in cost. They also come in sets at small savings. All you really need to do any of the projects in this book where a chisel may be of advantage is a 1-inch-wide wood chisel. Get the best you can find. It may run about $3, but it will hold a sharp edge longer. If you purchase one with a steel pommel—that is, the part of the handle that you will be striking with a mallet or hammer—the chisel should last many, many years.

A second additional tool which will be of help in smoothing wood is a plane. Basically, a plane is a chisel held at a certain angle in a handle, which can be guided along a piece of wood to shave off a very thin piece. It is much faster than sandpaper and, if used properly, will not round the edges of the wood should you desire them flat.

However, a plane is a rather tricky tool to use. If not perfectly aligned to the plane of the board, it will bevel the edge of the wood—that is, it will cut the edge at an angle. Also, the edge of the plane blade is quite thin, and the tiniest nick in the cutting edge will leave a ridge in the planed surface which must be sanded out. If you know how to use a plane, or are willing to take the time to experiment on scrap lumber until you get the technique right, then I recommend it highly. It does save time, and in educated hands does a marvelous job. If you don't want to take the time to practice, however, stay away from it, and save the money to buy extra wood for another project.

In some instances a cut will be very rough, and sanding would take too long to be practical. You don't really need a plane if you purchase a remarkable little tool called a Surform. These come in various styles, from plane shape to rasp shape, and even in round and half-round forms. A cross between a rasp and a plane, they can re-

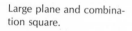

Large plane and combination square.

move wood at an amazing rate, taking an edge down to sanding level in just a few moments. A Surform won't leave the smooth surface that a plane will leave, but it is much simpler for the novice to use. It is also not as delicate, and should you dull or break a blade (about the only way you can do that is by beating it with a hammer) you can purchase replacement blades, usually for less than a $1. In fact, the whole tool, even in its largest sizes, seldom runs over $3 or $4, less than half the cost of a moderately good plane. I recommend it highly.

There are also a few small tools you might like to have on hand. The first is a screw starter. This is a shaft set in a handle, looking something like a screwdriver, only instead of a flat blade it has a sharp point and screw threads of increasing diameter. It is used, as its name implies, to make starting holes in wood for the screws to follow. In many cases, especially in softwood like pine, it eliminates the need to drill pilot holes. At a cost of less than $1, it is a worth-while investment.

A nail set is also handy. Whether called a punch, countersink, brad set, or some other name, it is designed to drive the head of a brad or finishing nail below the surface of the wood (countersink it) so that, when the resulting hole is filled with plastic wood, the head of the nail will be completely buried. In use, you drive the nail normally until the head protrudes only $1/8$ inch to $1/16$ inch from the surface. Then you place the nail set on the head of the nail, and strike it with the hammer until the head of the nail is countersunk. The nail sets come in different sizes, depending upon the size nails or brads to be used, but at approximately 50 cents apiece you can afford to have a couple. They help to give any nailed together project a much neater finished appearance.

POWER TOOLS

We started off with saws in the section on hand tools, so we'll do the same here. Two varieties of power saws for the handyman are of great advantage. The first, the circular saw, takes a circular blade approximately 7 inches in diameter (some are larger, some smaller). This saw replaces both the rip and the crosscut saw, and with a hollow-ground planer blade, it leaves a glass-smooth cut. But the circular saw starts at about $20 and goes up. For a person building furniture, it is a great aid; for the projects in this book, it is solely a convenience tool.

The second saw is the saber saw. A versatile piece of equipment, it can be used to cut straight lines, curves, and miters, and the price starts at $10. If you want a power saw, in my opinion this is the one

Circular saw and saber saw.

to start with. With the proper blades you can cut lumber up to 2 inches thick, and you can also cut intricate and long curves. Again, this is a handy tool, and very versatile, but actually nonessential for the projects in this book.

The third power tool has a lot to recommend it. This is the power drill. It replaces both the breast drill and the brace and bit, and is much handier to use. The wood bits, those which replace the large bits of the brace, are also less expensive than those for the brace, and can be purchased quite reasonably either in sets or singly as the need arises. But the greatest advantage is cost. Today, a ¼-inch power drill may be purchased for less than $10, a ⅜-inch drill for less than $12. If you can, get the ⅜-inch drill for its greater versatility. Don't worry about variable speeds or drills which reverse. You don't need a lot of gimmicks—just a good, serviceable drill.

There are other advantages to the power drill as well, in the line of available accessories. You can, as the need or the spirit moves you, add sanding disks, buffing wheels, hole saws (for holes larger than the drills can handle), screwdriving attachments, grinding wheels, and even devices which turn the drill into a small circular saw. The choice, and the variety, are both up to you, depending

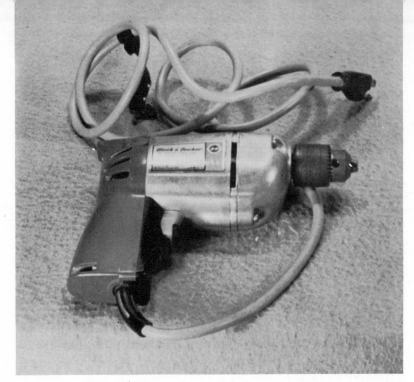

Power drill.

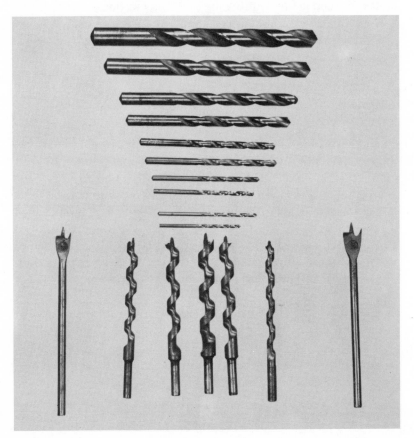

Bits for power drill.

upon your needs, your wishes, and your expense account. For our purposes, I strongly recommend the power drill in place of the two varieties of hand drills. It costs less than the two combined, and enables you to do so much more.

MATERIALS

Some materials you must have for all of the projects in this book; others are used less frequently. Where a piece of material is used on one project only, as in the case of the midge vise, that item is covered in the appropriate chapter. Each chapter has a proper listing of materials, in case you prefer to go individually, but since several projects can be made out of one small store of materials, some basic needs are listed here.

Wood is the primary material for all the projects in the book. This includes regular lumber as well as plywood. In some cases, plywood can be substituted for lumber, and I have indicated where this can be done in the individual chapters. It will be noted, however, that although plywood is in many cases easier to work with than lumber, the end grain, showing the plies and the glue joints, does not make as attractive a finished piece. The choice is up to you.

I have tried in most instances to keep the measurements of the larger projects to the dimensions of standard mill-cut lumber, or combinations thereof. At this point, a word should be said about those dimensions, in case you are not familiar with the system.

In the first place, boards are purchased by the running foot; that is, you pay a certain amount for each linear foot of the board, a price which increases as the width and/or thickness of the wood increases. Therefore, if a given width and thickness of lumber sells for 30 cents a foot, a 6-foot board would cost $1.80, an 8-foot board $2.40, and so on. The linear measurements are accurate.

Not so with width and thickness, however. Milled lumber does not actually measure the stated width and thickness. Nevertheless, it is standard. A table of common dimensions follows:

Stated (nominal) dimensions	Actual dimensions
$1 \times 2''$	$^{3}/_{4} \times 1^{1}/_{2}''$
$1 \times 3''$	$^{3}/_{4} \times 2^{1}/_{2}''$
$1 \times 4''$	$^{3}/_{4} \times 3^{1}/_{2}''$
$1 \times 6''$	$^{3}/_{4} \times 5^{1}/_{2}''$
$1 \times 8''$	$^{3}/_{4} \times 7^{1}/_{2}''$
$1 \times 10''$	$^{3}/_{4} \times 9^{1}/_{4}''$
$1 \times 12''$	$^{3}/_{4} \times 11^{1}/_{4}''$

In 2-inch lumber, the widths correspond to those of the 1-inch, and the thickness is 1½ inches. Therefore, an 8-foot length of 1 × 6-inch board would measure ¾ inch by 5½ inches by 8 feet; a 6-foot length of 2 × 8-inch board would measure 1½ inches by 7¼ inches by 6 feet. All stated plywood measurements are actual, and can be relied upon: ¾-inch plywood is truly ¾ inch thick.

Therefore, if I state the measurement of a project as being 18½ inches in height, and recommend the use of lumber, don't worry about cutting, because two 10-inch boards glued together will measure exactly 18½ inches, final measurement.

This takes care of the major materials. On the matter of fasteners, you will need a good supply of nails, for they are used most in the projects listed in this book. We will use two major types of nails—common and finishing. The common nail has a large head on it, and is excellent for major construction, especially when there will be stress against the joint; the finishing nail has a very small head, not very noticeable in a finished project. It can be driven into the wood, recessed with a punch, and filled over with putty to make it totally invisible.

Nails are classified in penny sizes (e.g., 6-penny nail), and the size designations often are abbreviated: 6d, etc. The lengths of various nails, as well as the approximate number per pound, are as follows:

Common nails			Finishing nails		
Size	Length	No. per pound	Size	Length	No. per pound
2d	1″	850	3d	1¼″	
3d	1¼″	545	4d	1½″	
4d	1½″	300	6d	2″	
5d	1¾″	250	8d	2½″	
6d	2″	175	10d	3″	
7d	2¼″	150			
8d	2½″	100			
9d	2¾″	90			
10d	3″	60			
12d	3¼″	55			
16d	3½″	42			
20d	4″	29			

Nails are sold by the pound. You should have on hand at least a pound of all sizes up through 6d, in both varieties. Any other sizes you can purchase as needed. The sole exception is in building the midge vise, which calls for a single 16d nail. Try this ploy, unless you want to build about 42 midge vises: If your hardware store sells nails loose (rather than prepackaged in 1- and 2-pound boxes), purchase all your other nails at once, then put a wistful look on your face, and say that you need only one 16d nail. If you are lucky, the clerk will give you a conspiratorial wink, and hand you one. Or maybe he will just add one into the total weight of one of the other lots of nails.

Screws come next on the list of fasteners and they go by actual length, ranging in size from ¼ inch to 3 inches in length. Do *not* buy an assortment, no matter how attractive the price is. You won't use over a third of the screws they palm off on you as an "all-round assortment." Screws can be purchased singly, or in packages of four to six depending upon the size, so just buy them as needed, and as specified in the bills of materials for the individual projects.

Another point on screws. Most of these projects are meant to be used in the field. Therefore, although brass screws cost up to three times as much as steel screws of the same size, buy the brass! They won't rust, they won't corrode, and, especially when brass fittings are used, as on the wooden tackle box or the custom-fitted shotgun case, the brass makes a beautiful and rich finish. You won't need that many brass screws for the projects listed here, and they are well worth the extra cost.

The final fastener you need is glue. Buy the best, as a glue that gives way in the middle of nowhere is worthless. White glue such as Elmer's is fine, although the brand of white glue known as Weldbond is thicker, and seems to work better for me. Stay away from such things as contact cement and model-airplane glue; they don't serve the purpose in these projects. All wood joints, even if nails and screws are used to hold them together, should be glued as well. It makes a much stronger bond, and a waterproof joint as well.

Well, that's about it. A few other materials will be mentioned as needed, but with some of the above on hand, you are ready to build a fair number of the projects in the book. So turn to something that looks good, and let's get to work.

II

FOR
THE FISHERMAN

3
Camera Case for Fishermen

Certainly one of the greatest joys of a fishing trip, or of any sporting trip, for that matter, is in the memories of special events which occurred, mulled over weeks, months, or even years later in front of a blazing fire, with a drink and a pipe in hand. In fact, I think that it is in anticipation of such evenings that many people go on fishing trips in the first place. And nothing can recall those special events as vividly as an album of good photos of the trip. Yes, good pictures help bring back the memories; but if there is one thing more delicate than a No. 22 Quill Gordon, it's the mechanism of a camera. The least little bit of the elements can rupture the insides of a good camera as quickly as a hammer can. Water, grit, spray, and jouncing, all may leave the photographic fisherman with a camera mechanism that either grinds, jingles when it is moved, or won't move at all.

The common photographer's gadget bags do not really protect a camera and lenses along a stream or in a boat. They are merely carrying cases, which protect gear from a mild rain, but are worthless when a boat swamps or the fisherman does a half-gainer off a slippery bank into an icy stream. Also, they are not cushioned, and the jouncing of a boat as it goes from one comber to the next is harder on the insides of a camera than it is on the bottom of a fisherman.

Since I carry a camera with me whenever I go fishing—proper illustration for articles is a great part of my livelihood—I developed a fitted camera case that protects all the equipment I normally need from both hard knocks and moisture. It is perhaps the easiest project in the entire book, and one which can be quite valuable, as camera repairs are very costly.

The bill of materials is very short, but not the least expensive:

BILL OF MATERIALS	
1	discarded metal tackle box
2	3"-thick foam rubber
	(size to fit snugly in tackle box)

You may already have an old metal tackle box lying around; if not, make the camera case and then you'll have an excuse to build the wooden tackle box in Chapter 8. If you don't have an old metal tackle box, then buy one. You can pick one up that will do quite nicely for about $3 at any of the discount department stores. The notions department of the department store carries the foam rubber.

Once you've got the foam and the box, you're over halfway there. With a pair of heavy scissors, cut the foam so that you have two pieces just slightly larger than the inside of the tackle box. Since these boxes vary in size, I offer no dimensions for this operation.

Now, very carefully pry the cantilever tray loose from the tackle box, trying not to dent or bend the box. Should any of the rivets pull through the sides of the box, pick up a tube of metal putty, the sort that is commonly used on auto body repairs, and fill in the holes. This will keep the box waterproof.

Coat the inside bottom and sides of the box with white glue, and press one of the pieces of foam rubber into the box. Do NOT use any other type of glue for this operation, because the chemical constituents of some glues will attack the foam rubber itself, and all you'll end up with is a sodden mass of glop in the bottom of the box.

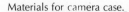
Materials for camera case.

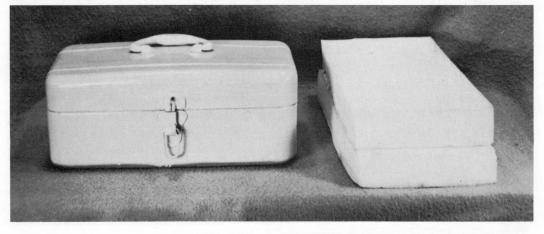

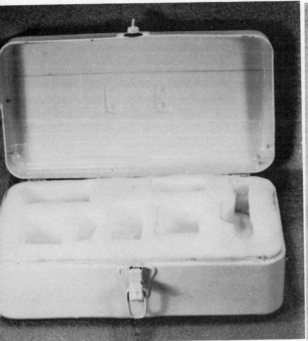

Foam cut out and in place.   The finished product.

Now, take the camera gear that you wish to carry into the field, and lay it out on the remaining piece of foam rubber. Here again, the size of the box will determine the amount of gear you can fit into it. My own case measures $7 \times 14 \times 5$ inches, and with it I can carry a 35mm camera body, a 35mm wide-angle lens, a 135mm telephoto lens, a battery-powered electronic flash unit, a variable close-up lens, a 2X telextender, and three filters. You can't ask for more than that, since the telextender gives me, in effect, four lenses—35mm, 70mm, 135mm, and 270mm—and the variable close-up lens, which screws onto the front of the 135 tele, enables me to fill the negative with something the size of a dragonfly.

With the equipment neatly laid out on the foam, and leaving ³/₄ inch of rubber minimum between each piece of equipment, take a felt-tipped marking pen (fine-line) and draw a line around each of the pieces. Cock the pen at a slight inward angle, so that the outline is just a bit smaller than the equipment itself. This will make the rubber hold each separate piece of gear tightly.

Now, with a razor blade or a very sharp pocketknife, cut all the way through the foam rubber. Be careful to keep the cuts perpendicular, or the equipment will not fit properly.

Take the section of foam, after all the cutouts have been made, and coat one side and all the edges thickly with white glue. Be careful not to get any in any of the compartments. Wait until the glue gets tacky, then glue the section into the box on top of the solid piece. If the box is extremely deep, glue enough foam into the top of the box so that the equipment makes contact with it. If it is shallow, as mine is, there is no need for any rubber in the top.

When the glue is thoroughly dry, fit the pieces of equipment into their respective compartments, and you're ready to go. The lips that tackle boxes have to keep water out work very well for camera cases, and with the air-cell construction of the foam rubber, even with the added weight of the camera equipment, the box will float if it falls overboard.

4
Midge Vise

Several years ago, when I first began fly-fishing, I purchased all my flies. As I am given to losing them on the backcast as well as to fish, I soon began tying my own. Not only did this cut the expense considerably, it also enabled me to develop a few patterns of my own which seemed to work better on the waters I fished than any I could find in the major shops.

However, I soon ran into the problem that most fly-tiers face eventually. The standard vises on the market today are excellent for hook sizes down to about No. 12, but with anything smaller they become awkward. And when tying flies in Nos. 18 to 22, they become well-nigh impossible. So I was faced with the choice between making do and buying the smaller flies so necessary for low-water fishing.

Something of the Scotsman in me rebelled at the latter, but I couldn't produce a well-made small fly with an impractically large vise. The only alternative was to create a vise small enough to handle the work. The results of that experiment I call the midge vise.

The midge vise must have certain characteristics in order to be effective. First, the jaws must be small enough to permit maximum exposure of the hook shank. Secondly, the jaws must be able to hold the hook firmly without damaging the fine wire in the smallest sizes.

The vise also should adjust to angle so that a fly can be examined while it is still in the vise. It should be small enough so that it can be carried to the streamside along with a small selection of materials, permitting the fisherman to match any hatches he happens to run across. And because sportsmen in general have a tendency to spend more money on their hobby than is compatible with marital harmony, it should be inexpensive and easy to build.

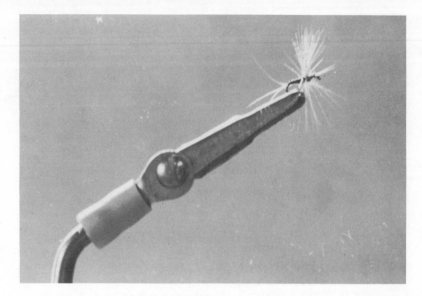

Fly in the midge vise.

Filling all of these needs at once may seem almost as difficult as trying to tie a No. 22 Quill Gordon in a machinist's vise, but actually, they can all be achieved rather easily.

The components may already be in the fly-fisher's workshop, but if not, even the smallest hardware stores carry them.

BILL OF MATERIALS		
1	16d common nail	vise shank
1	solderless wire terminal for 10- to 12-gauge wire	vise pivot
1	Series 70 alligator clip	vise jaws
1	1 × 2″ pine, 2″ long	base

Even if you have none of these components at home, the total cost of the parts is somewhere in the neighborhood of a quarter.

Once you have the components, construction of the vise itself is simple and requires few tools. In fact, a hammer, a screwdriver, emery cloth or a file, a hacksaw or pair of wire cutters, and a pair of pliers are all that you need, although a vise makes the second step a bit easier and a little more accurate.

First drive the 16d nail through the center of the block of wood. Finding the center is relatively simple: take a ruler, and connect the points of the block with the points opposite them on the diagonal

The makings of a midge vise.

with a pencil line. The result will be an "X" on the block, and the intersection of the "X" is the exact center of the wooden base. Since driving a nail of that size through a relatively small block risks splitting the wood, drill a pilot hole first, $\frac{1}{8}$ inch in diameter, completely through the block. Now rub the nail along the side of your nose. The natural oils at the side of your nose will lubricate the nail, and it will penetrate much easier. Professional carpenters use this trick in laying hardwood floors. Drive the nail through the pilot hole, far enough so that the head countersinks; otherwise the vise will wobble. With the pilot hole and the lubricated nail, countersinking the head is quite simple.

Then, place the nail, point first, into the vise; or, if you don't have a vise, grasp it with a pair of pliers. Bend the nail approximately $\frac{3}{4}$ inch from the point, and make an angle of about 60 degrees with the base. These guidelines, however, are not crucial to the effectiveness of the finished vise.

Now grip the flat part of the solderless wire connector with the pliers or with the vise and, using another nail, open up the wire channel so that the nail makes a tight friction fit. Remove the connector and force it down over the point of the bent nail.

Now we turn to the alligator clip. The two points or ears on the back of the clip, in its normal use, are designed to be clamped over the wire it is fastened to. For our purposes, these must be removed. If they are not, they will snag the fine silk used with the small flies. These ears must be cut off with a hacksaw or a pair of wire cutters. Do not try to break them off—this will leave a jagged edge that will

Bending the nail.

Wire connector fitted on point of nail.

File the teeth of the alligator clip.

The midge vise adjusts to many positions.

do just as much damage to the silk as the ears themselves. Touch up the cut with a file or emery cloth.

While you have the file or the emery cloth in your hand, run it over the teeth of the alligator clip several times. We need the teeth for superior gripping power, but we do not want them too sharp because they might damage the finish on the hook or the hook wire itself.

Now, remove the screw from the alligator clip, put it through the hole in the solderless connector, and attach the clip to the other side.

The vise is finished.

The terminal, if desired, may be soldered onto the nail, but I have not found such an operation necessary. And by loosening and tightening the screw in the side, the angle of the jaws may be readily adjusted. The alligator clip, thanks to the serrated jaws, holds the small hooks quite firmly, although the vise is too small for hooks much larger than No. 6. But then, this is a specialized tool, and we always have our larger vise for the streamer patterns, bugs, and whatever else we happen to need.

If you have to purchase a package of alligator clips in order to get one, and you would rather tie some midges than make up extra vises for your fishing partners, prop the jaws of the clips open, squeeze in a little liquid rubber, level it off even with the points of the teeth, and let it set up overnight. The clips make excellent small hackle pliers when treated in this manner; and if you screw one to a small block of wood you will have a small tool to hold your tying thread under tension while you attend to other operations.

Incidentally, while the midge vise can be carried "as is" to the streamside, there is an alternative construction method made to order for streamside use. In this method, instead of sinking the nail through a block of wood, simply saw the head off the nail and epoxy the shank into the end of a 6-inch length of dowel rod. Then you can hold the vise firmly between your knees at the streamside, leaving both hands free for tying. And when the fish are rising to a fly that you can't duplicate out of your fly boxes, you need all the hands you can get.

So there it is: a fully adjustable midge vise that you can make yourself with a minimum of tools—and it only costs a quarter. The instructions take far longer to read than to follow. So try one, and see if the next time you are tying some No. 18 Ginger Quills things don't go more easily and more accurately.

5
Streamside Fly-Tying Kit

How many times have you stood on the bank of a stream and watched the fish rising in a sheer orgy of feeding to a hatch you could easily identify, but couldn't duplicate from your fly boxes? If you are anything like me this has happened more times than you like to remember. Then there are the times when the fish are feeding beautifully and a 4-pound brown not only takes your last fly of the immediate pattern, but nonchalantly starts feeding again an easy cast away. It almost makes you glad you have so many appropriate Anglo-Saxon words at your disposal.

At any rate, we are undoubtedly more contented when such an event does not occur. For fly-tiers the problem can be easily avoided simply by carrying some tools and materials to the streamside.

Now, before you start, I know full well that a fly-tier accumulates so much in materials and tools that he would need a Ford van to carry it all to the stream. But look at the situation. You are not going to be tying Jock Scotts and Black Ghosts at streamside. You will not, in fact, even be tying the attractor patterns. Rather, you will be matching the hatch, and, if you fish a stream with any consistency, you know what patterns are most likely to be found there. In addition, the materials used for imitator patterns are really quite similar; some can be substituted in a pinch, and if you're trying to tie a pattern before a hatch stops, let's face it, you are in a pinch.

No, the materials themselves are not a problem. But the tools, and the means of transporting the tools and materials to the stream, do pose a slight problem. And solving that problem is the purpose of this chapter.

Obviously, the streamside fly-tying kit must have certain characteristics. It has to be easily portable, because a fisherman festooned

A handy item, the stream-side fly-tying kit.

with set-up rod, creel, and net does not really need any great encumbrance when fighting his way through the greenbrier to his favorite stream. It must therefore be small and light. It must also be efficient in its storage of materials, for the same reason. There cannot be any wasted space. And, finally, it must be inexpensive. Have you ever dropped anything into a fast-moving trout stream, and watched it bob gaily out of sight around the bend—or over a spillway?

There is a way to get around all of these difficulties quite easily—a lunch box. Don't use the metal variety, because these will rust out after a few seasons, and they are not waterproof, so the materials inside could easily get wet if the box took a spill into the stream. I for one do not relish trying to tie an accurate fly with a soggy feather.

However, the newer vinyl lunch boxes are made to order for our purposes. They are light in weight, the vinyl will take the fasteners that are needed to transform the container from lunch box to kit, and they also have what amounts to a tongue-and-groove lip that effectively seals out water should the box take a tumble. If you drop it into the stream open, you're hopeless anyway, so don't worry about it. And the boxes are available at discount drug and department stores for around $3.

BILL OF MATERIALS

1	1" pine, 4½" square	divider
1	½" pine, 5" wide and 12" long	large compartment cover
1	½ × 7 × 4½" plywood	hook rack
12	½" roundhead brass screws	
2	small brass hinges	
1	small brass hasp/latch	
2	compartmented plastic boxes	
6	35mm film cans	
1	small wooden knob	

Just about everything in the list can be found at the local hardware store. Plastic boxes are sold in a variety of stores—department stores, sewing shops, etc. The little aluminum film cans that 35mm film is packed in may be a bit more of a problem if you don't happen to take your own photographs, but there are several ways around it. The first is to stop by your local camera shop. Someone there undoubtedly uses a 35mm camera, and since the cans are usually thrown away, he will probably give you as many as you like. Or, if

Materials for fly-tying kit.

all else fails, your druggist will probably give you some plastic pill vials, or sell you some quite cheaply. If you have to go the pill-vial route, however, you will have to make an adjustment in construction technique. I'll explain it later.

With all the materials at hand, the construction of the kit is not very difficult at all. The first step is to partition off the bottom to make a tool compartment and a compartment for the plastic boxes, which will contain the small materials. Measure over 7 inches from the right-hand side of the box as it faces you, and with the point of a nail, scribe a line across the bottom of the box and up both of the long sides. Now, measure the inside bottom and the inside top of the box, and the distances across at those points. Lay out those measurements on the $1 \times 4\frac{1}{2} \times 4\frac{1}{2}$-inch piece, and cut it so that it slides into the box. These boxes taper toward the bottom, and there appears to be no standard taper, so the dimensions of this piece depend upon the individual box.

Place this divider in the bottom of the box, and affix it firmly with two brass screws in each side. Set the two plastic boxes in beside it. Now, take the $\frac{1}{2} \times 7 \times 4\frac{1}{2}$-inch piece of plywood, and either clamp it to the top of your workbench or pin it there with a finishing nail so that it will be held rigidly. Drilling the holes with a $1\frac{1}{4}$-inch bit exerts quite a bit of torque on the wood, and if the board isn't held securely you'll never get through it.

Divider in place, with room for compartmented plastic boxes.

The knob, which is necessary so that the hook rack can be lifted out to gain access to the small materials compartment, cannot be centered due to the width of the cans, so it must be offset. Also, the arrangement of the cans can be done differently if you wish to experiment, but don't get carried away, because the size of the board limits the number of cans that can be effectively utilized. If they are too close together, you won't be able to unscrew the lids without removing the can from the rack entirely, and that both wastes time and puts stress on the wood between the cans. My own box contains six cans, which I have found to be enough. For the sake of description, therefore, I will explain the arrangement of the hook rack that I have found to be most efficient, and let you proceed from that point. If you use pill vials of smaller diameter, you will be able to fit more of them into the rack, and in a different pattern, but, again, don't get carried away. Too many will weaken the rack and make removal of hooks for tying quite awkward.

Now comes the point where there may need to be some modifications. If you use the film cans there is no problem. Simply drill six 1¼-inch holes through the wood with the brace and bit. This will make a nice friction fit for the cans. Push them through the holes, and the lips of the cans will catch on the holes, keeping the cans from going all the way through. Pill vials, however, come in a wide variety of sizes, and so I can give you no standard hole sizes for them. You will have to measure them and proceed from there.

Now, take the can rack, and set it on top of the plastic boxes. It should fit nicely over them, and the friction fit of the cans prevents them from popping up. These are the hook containers, individually

Hook rack. Don't try to fit too many cans in the rack. Six is all this piece of wood can take.

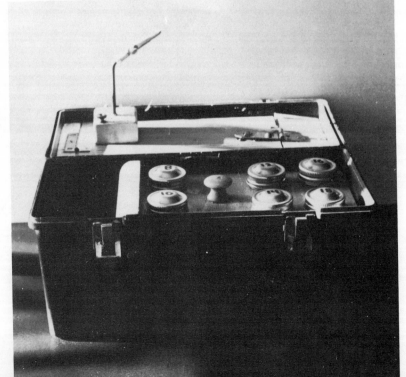

The kit, complete with midge vise.

removable and, thanks to the seal of the cans, waterproof. Write the size numbers of the hooks you are carrying on the lids of the cans with a waterproof marking pen.

The large material compartment is simple to finish off. Cut the board to the exact size of the top of the box. Now, off one end, cut a piece 1 inch wide; off the other, a piece 2 inches wide. Screw the 1-inch piece to the left inside end of the box, the 2-inch piece to the right inside end. At the left end of the large leftover piece, center and affix the hinge, and then place the unit into the top of the box and affix the other side of the hinge to the 1-inch left-hand piece. Mount the latch on the 2-inch end piece, and its hasp on the long board so that it latches with just a wee bit of friction, to keep it from swinging open in transit. The box has now become a Streamside Fly-tying Kit.

As for tools, the midge vise described in the previous chapter is an excellent vise to carry along, since it fits right down into the tool compartment of the bottom. Add to this a small pair of scissors and a pair of hackle pliers, and you have all the tools you need.

As for materials, they more or less depend upon your area's needs. Just as a starting point, however, the materials that I carry are as follows:

Hooks: Nos. 8, 10, 12, 14, 16, 18.

In small material compartment: 1 spool black tying thread; floss assortment; chenille assortment; peacock herl; plastic junglecock eyes; brown, gray, and green wool; muskrat and fox fur; and a few already stripped quills.

In large material compartment: 1 natural bucktail; 1 yellow calftail; 1 pair starling wings; 1 pair grouse wings; 1 pair matched duck primary feathers each in gray, black, and white; and 3 envelopes of brown, black, and red hackles.

That's it. And the kit is still by no means full. Try one out, and see if your next fishing trip isn't a little less frustrating when a big brown rises to a black gnat and, in the middle of a careful cast to him, your last gnat is eaten by that big willow tree behind you.

6

The Wilson Eel

I suppose all of us want immortality in one way or another. Some of us seek it through children; I'm looking for it through an eel. An eel fly, that is.

The eel is one of the staples of most saltwater fishes' diets. But eels are expensive to use as bait, and they don't cast well with a 4-ounce fly rod. Not at all well. So I decided that if I was to take proper advantage of the opportunities for fly-fishing in the Chesapeake Bay and tidal rivers around it, I would have to create a representation of an eel with so close a resemblance that fish would not be able to tell the difference.

The result was this fly, which has accounted for more striped bass and bluefish than any other fly in my saltwater collection. As the optimum length for live eels in most saltwater fishing is between 4 and 8 inches, the pattern described here strikes the medium at 6 inches. By using different-sized hooks the fly can be increased or decreased in size at will.

The fly is, in effect, a tandem streamer, but its form, method of tying, and coloration make it particularly effective.

The Wilson eel.

```
                            BILL OF MATERIALS

  2          #4, 3X long-shanked hooks                    Tandem hook
  2          3" lt. metallic blue saddle hackles
  1          6" length lt. gray chenille
  4          5" black saddle hackles
  1          4" white saddle hackle
  1          5" dark green saddle hackles
             black thread
             head cement (or nail polish)
```

Take a No. 4 3X long-shanked hook, and put it in your vise. At the bend, tie in two light metallic blue saddle hackles, 3 inches in length. Also at this point, tie in a length of light gray chenille, wind it to ⅛ inch behind the eye, and tie it off. At the eye, tie in two black saddle hackles, long enough to overlap two-thirds of the metallic blue hackles. Whip-finish, lacquer the head, and put this hook aside to dry.

Now take a second hook of the same size and place it in the vise. At the bend, tie in another length of silver gray chenille, wind it forward to ¼ inch behind the eye, and tie it off.

Here is the tricky part. Take a 4-inch dark metallic green saddle hackle, and tie it in so that it lies flat along the top of the chenille. This is the back of the eel. Next, take a 3-inch-long white saddle hackle, and tie it in so that it lies flat along the bottom of the chenille and extends past the bend of the hook to form the eel's belly. Now, take two 5-inch-long black saddle hackles, and tie them in, one on either side of the hook, taking care not to cock the back and belly feathers. But when you are tying them in, do not use the normal method of opposing the curves of the hackle ribs. Rather, tie them in so that both hackles curve in the same direction. This curve will cause the fly to undulate in the water like a living eel. Tie off the head, making it full, lacquer it, and force the point of the hook through the eye of the first hook you tied. Arrange the feathers so that they overlap smoothly. In the water the combination of these colors duplicates the colors of the living eel almost exactly—at least, closely enough to fool an awful lot of fish.

You may want to paint eyes on the head of the fly for greater effectiveness. By all means do so if it makes the fly more attractive to you. I have fished with them both ways, and can tell no difference in effectiveness, so I generally leave them off.

At any rate, give the fly a try. In smaller sizes, replacing the black feathers with brown, the fly also serves in fresh water as a lamprey imitation. And when your friends look upon your success with justifiable awe, give me a taste of immortality, and tell them you could only have done it with the Wilson Eel.

7

Emergency
Fly Dressings

For the fly-tier, with his multitudinous boxes of flies and a streamside fly-tying kit, there is no problem with the availability of flies. But for the fly-fisherman who does not tie his own, for the plug or spinner fisherman who comes upon trout rising to mayflies, or for the fisherman who has his tackle box lost or stolen with several days still to go on his trip—for these people there is an advantage in knowing how to create an acceptable, if not beautiful, lure with the materials they can find around them.

Let's take the plug or spinner fisherman first, because right from his tackle box he can create several flyweight lures which can draw fish. I do wish to make the statement, however, that several of the lures made in this manner would not be classed legally as flies, and should *not* be used on fly-fishing-only streams. If you are hurt, or lost, and without food, you aren't interested in flies in that sense, and can use any lures or bait you have in your box. The emergency fly dressings here are listed in order to help a fisherman more fully enjoy or diversify his sport when he cannot obtain proper flies.

Many plug and spinner fishermen have either pork rind or salmon eggs in their tackle boxes, and these can be turned into devastating "streamer flies" with just a little ingenuity. First thread several salmon eggs on a long-shanked hook, forcing the point of the hook through the eggs and then sliding them along the shank toward the head. Then cut narrow strips of the pork rind with your pocketknife, two long and one short. With your fishing line, tie the short piece on at the bend of the hook for a tail, and the two long pieces side by side at the eye of the hook for the wings. It's heavy, a little difficult to cast, and it really is bait, but it is bait used to its greatest effectiveness; for the spin fisherman, it can be fished quite well by

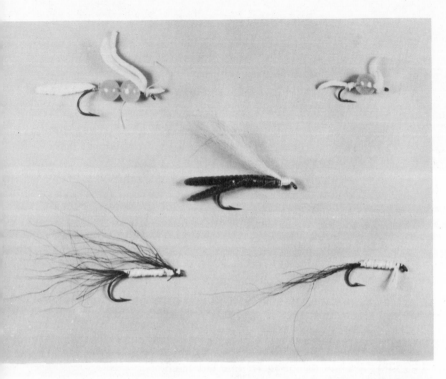

Some emergency fly dressings.

tying it on a 6-foot leader and using either a clear plastic bubble or a regular float for the casting weight. Because of the consistency of the salmon eggs, the "streamer" is not very durable, but it will catch fish, and the "wings" and "tail" help to keep the eggs from sliding one way or the other on the hook.

Smaller wet flies can be made in the same manner, using one egg on a small hook for the body and three short (¼- to ½-inch) pieces of pork rind, one for the tail, and two cocked for the wings. This is easier to cast with a fly rod, but definitely requires a bubble for any other sort of fishing.

Another highly effective fly can be made if the fisherman has a few plastic worms and some lead-head jigs in his box. Cut the hair off one of the jigs, and tie it around the eye of the hook, making enough turns of the fishing line to get the effect of a bulky head. Now break off a piece of a plastic worm slightly longer than the hair, and thread it fully onto the hook. With the pocketknife, split the end of the worm so that it comes away from the bend of the hook and extends straight back past the bend. The split will give the "fly" a scissorlike, swimming action in the water. Like the egg-and-rind flies, this variety can also be made into a wet fly by using a much shorter piece of worm for the body, and adding a bit of the hair from the jig for a tail as well as wings.

Some emergency fly dressings, however, can be used on fly-fishing-only streams, because nothing in them is or could be used as a natural bait. These are flies that anyone can make with the materials right at hand, and, while they are in no way attractive to the fisherman's eye, they apparently affect fish differently. I have tested them all and, while they will never be outlawed because of their effectiveness, they will catch fish at times, and they can save the day when a fly-fisherman does a swan dive off a high bank and watches his fly boxes float off down the river.

Flies are primarily some cloth body material and hair or feathers. Well, you're wearing cloth and you have hair on your head, unless you're bald, in which case you should grow a beard.

The patterns that are available are few, but they work. Simply take a strip of cloth, or unravel a length of thread from the tail of your shirt or the top of your sock. The sock is better, since it is usually both stronger and bulkier. Use that thread both for making the body and for tying on the wings and tail, both of which are made from strands of your own hair.

Fly-tiers pay good money for raffia, a dried African grass used for fly bodies. Regular marsh grass makes a nice golden or insect-green substitute. Use hair for the wings and tail again.

Well, that's it. Nothing fancy, no world-beaters, and certainly not beautiful. But then, I knew a woman once who was so ugly she had to creep up on a glass to get a drink of water, but she was a good cook. These flies are just about that ugly, but they will catch fish.

8
Wooden
Tackle Box

Have you ever looked with envy at those pictures of fishermen in England and Scotland with their beautifully designed split bamboo rods, delicate and perfectly balanced reels, and those rich and handsome looking wooden tackle boxes with the brass fittings? Have you ever priced one of those tackle boxes through the few elite sportsman's catalogs that offer them? And, having done so, haven't you then decided that it would really be better to pay off the mortgage on the house or have the child's teeth straightened?

Well, friend Cassius, put away your lean and hungry look, because now you can build one for less than $5. The only difficulties you will face are that the box will take several hours to construct properly, and that should you have to do it on the weekends or during the evenings, you may not have the time for more enjoyable pursuits such as taking out the garbage. And, if you happen to hunt as well, some of the construction aspects of the tackle box will serve you again when it comes to building the custom-fitted shotgun case in Chapter 19.

There are certain advantages and disadvantages to having a wooden tackle box. The advantages are that you can adapt it to your own special needs, that the smaller boxes have an elite appearance; and that, if you are a plastic worm fisherman who has had tackle-box trays dissolve on contact with the soft plastic baits, wooden trays are completely wormproof. The disadvantages are that the wooden boxes outweigh comparable-sized boxes of plastic or aluminum; and that, as the box increases in size, it loses some of the class of the smaller boxes and becomes ungainly. This last is especially true in the large boxes needed for saltwater casting; it is partially outweighed, in a practical if not in an aesthetic sense, by the large wooden box's ability to "live" in the boat, unaffected by saltwater corrosion, and take harder knocks without splitting or denting out of shape as will tackle boxes of other materials.

To at least attempt to please everybody, rather than give the plans for one sort of tackle box, I will give plans for two varieties: one elite, very attractive box for the fly-fisherman or spin fisherman, whose lures are smaller and who requires an attractive and portable box; and a second, larger box, designed as a boat box for the salt-water fisherman who requires a functional, heavy-duty tackle box designed to hold massive lures.

THE SPINNING BOX

The construction details of this box, the more elite of the two, are far trickier than those of the boat box. They have to be to accomplish the smooth grace which this sort of box should have. This box

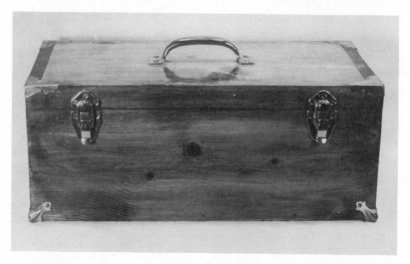

The elite spinning box.

will be slightly heavier than a comparable one of professional manufacture, because the professionals have sophisticated power equipment which can reduce their lumber to ½ inch in thickness, while we will be working with standard 1-inch lumber which actually measures ¾ inch in thickness. The bill of materials is as follows, in nominal rather than actual dimensions:

BILL OF MATERIALS

2	1 × 8″ pine, 18″ long	sides
2	1 × 8″ pine, 7½″ long	ends
2	1 × 8″ pine, 16½″ long	top and bottom
5	¼ × 7½ × 12″ plywood	tray bottoms
2	1 × 2″ pine, 8′ long	tray sides
3	¼ × 1″ lattice strip, 8′ long	tray dividers
2	¼ × 5″ quarter-round molding	tray guides
1	large brass door handle	
2	3″ brass hinges	
2	brass latches	
8	medium brass box corners	
24	1½″ flat hard brass screws	
1	pkg. ½″ brads	
½ lb.	3d finishing nails	
	white glue	
	wood filler	
	stain	
	varnish or Zar	

Before we begin construction, there are a few points to be made. To make this box into the elite sort of construction that we want, the joints must fit as smoothly as possible, with no gaps. Sadly enough, most lumber gains a slight warp in drying. Choose your lumber carefully, and pick the flattest board possible; carry along a metal ruler and lay the edge across the board, checking the gap in between the center of the board and the edge of the ruler to make sure you get the board with the least deviation.

The most perfect way of putting the box together would be through the use of miter joints. But to describe such a method would be making two unnecessary assumptions: first, that you have been able to find perfectly flat lumber; and second, that you have the proper power tools to make the necessarily precise miter cuts. If the cuts are not absolutely precise the mitered box will look worse than a properly finished box with butt joints, and if the wood is not perfectly flat you cannot get acceptable miters no matter how precisely you cut them. So I have elected to use butt joints. The box will take more care in final finishing, but construction is assured. Incidentally, one of the most attractive commercial wooden boxes I have seen was made of ½-inch mahogany put together with butt joints, and cost $85.

Now we can begin construction. With all of the pieces laid out in front of you, assemble the ends and sides of the box with the end pieces inside the sides. You will note that the end pieces are square, since the actual measurement of 8-inch lumber is 7½ inches, and that there will be two "cut" sides, showing the saw marks and open, or end, grain, and two "milled" sides, showing the planed surface smoothed by the mill. Place the ends so that the milled sides are at the top and bottom of the box, and the cut ends butt up against the sides of the box. Then, when it comes to the final finishing, only four cut ends will need to be reduced to the smoothness of the rest of the box. Assemble the butt joints with glue and brass screws; place one screw ½ inch from the top of the box, another ½ inch from the bottom, and two others evenly spaced between them. The reason for this positioning will become evident in a moment.

Now install the top and bottom of the box. You will note that the top and bottom fit into the box. This makes the finished product more attractive and easier to finish properly, since all the cut ends of the top and bottom are hidden by milled wood. The easiest means of installing these pieces is to coat all four edges with glue, place the piece flat on the workbench, and slide the box down over it. Then screw it together with wood screws, two in each end and four in each side. Do *not* try dropping the first piece through—that will smear glue all over the inside of the box. Now coat the edges of the second piece with glue, turn the box over, and perform the same operation over again. The body of the box is now complete. Let the glue dry overnight.

Mistake! you say. Now I have a box, but I can't get into it. You will be able to, as soon as the glue is dry. The reason for building the box in this manner is to make certain that the top and bottom will line up perfectly. In my salad days I built several boxes and their lids separately. None of them fitted right. Then a professional cabinet-maker showed me the trick of building the whole thing as a cube, and I haven't had any trouble since.

Now, after the glue is dry, take the box and measure down 1¼ inches from the top, all the way around. Make at least four measurements to the side, making a mark each time. Then take a ruler and join all of the points you have marked. If you have measured precisely, the lines should meet exactly at each of the four corners, making a solid line all the way around the box, 1¼ inches down from the top. If the lines don't meet precisely, remeasure, draw another line, and keep doing it until they do coincide. This step is crucial, and cannot be emphasized too strongly.

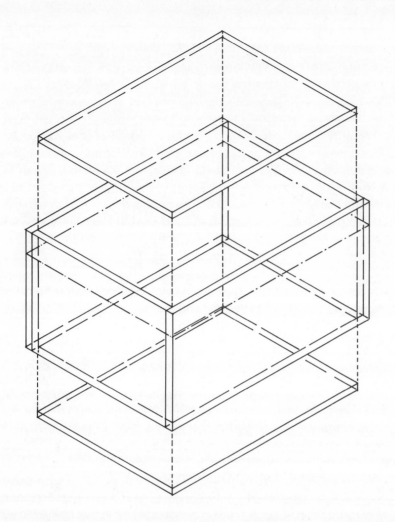

Exploded view of box construction. This is the basic method of building a box used in all box projects.

Once the line is precise, take either a carpenter's crosscut saw or a power saw, and begin to saw carefully through the box. One point, here: do not use a power jigsaw or saber saw as they are sometimes called. The blade is too narrow and will not keep a straight line, and the last thing in the world that you need is a tackle box with a scalloped edge. The crosscut or the power circular saw are the only two that will work. Go slowly! You've invested quite a bit of time in this already, and a slip here can ruin it. Make absolutely certain that the saw follows *both* the line on the end and the line on the side at the same time. When the saw reaches the bottom of the end piece, turn the construction over and start cutting through the other side, allowing the slot already in the end to help guide the blade. Still go slowly, so that the blade doesn't tear the end slot. When the blade reaches the bottom of the cut end again, proceed with the cutting, allowing the slot on the other side, which is now on the bottom, to help guide the blade. Keep going slowly, and cut all the way through the box. Now you see the reason for the positioning of the screws—with the measurements of the box and lid, placing the screws in the prescribed manner eliminates any possibility of striking one of them with the saw blade.

When the saw finally comes all the way through, you will have in effect two trays, the shallow one being the lid of the box and the deeper one being the bottom. Now sand the box thoroughly, inside and out. Use particular care on the cut ends of the sides which show at the ends of the box. These must be reduced to the same smoothness as the rest of the box. The best method is to start out with 50 grit paper, just on the cut ends, and work down until you reach 120 grit paper. Then go over the entire box with 120 and finally 220 grit garnet paper, and then with steel wool. This procedure will take a long time, so be patient. When you sand the cut edges where the lid fits onto the box, wrap the paper around a square block of wood to avoid beveling any of the edges of the joint.

Once the tackle box is perfectly smooth, inside and out, align the lid with the bottom of the box and mount two 3-inch brass hinges along one of the sides. Now you no longer have to worry about the alignment of the box—the hinges will hold it while you finish it up. Since you won't be bothering with the box while you work on the trays, now is the best time to apply the finish. This will give it a good chance to dry.

A box of this sort deserves a finish that will bring out the richness of the wood grain. The box in its present condition, being made of white pine, will be very light in color. Feel free to apply a good grade of stain if you prefer the darker woods. The stain should contain wood filler; that is, a component of the stain which will help fill the pores of the wood to give a smoother finish. Should you desire to leave the wood in its natural color, there are many excellent neutral wood fillers which will seal the wood pores without changing the color of the box.

The wood filler can be brushed on, but the stain-filler gives a much better finish when wiped on with a soft, lint-free cloth. The stain goes on much more evenly, and you can repeat applications after the stain dries to darken the wood to your own taste. No matter how smooth you sanded the wood, the application of the liquid stain and/or filler will raise the grain again. These fine hairs of the wood must be removed by rubbing with steel wool after each coat of stain has dried. Stain both the inside and outside of the box, so that the pores on the inside are filled and polished smooth as well—moisture from drying lures will penetrate the smallest exposed portion, causing the wood to swell unevenly.

Once the wood has been filled and/or stained and smoothed, apply at least three coats of a good grade marine or exterior varnish. Allow each coat to dry. After the second and third coats go over the box with 000 steel wool to remove any slight imperfections. Make the coats of varnish light and as smooth as possible, making certain that you blend in any accidental runs before the varnish has set. If you follow this rather time-consuming procedure exactly, the finished product should have the sheen and texture of glass.

Incidentally, there is a superb product on the market called Zar, available at most of the larger hardware stores. It is a crystal-clear acrylic finish, treated and applied in exactly the same manner as varnish. It is the toughest stuff I have ever seen—you can drop a hammer on a finished piece of wood, and although the wood will dent, the Zar finish will not crack or scrape. And it has the added advantage of never yellowing as many varnishes do when exposed to air and direct sunlight over a long period of time. It is more expensive than varnish, and since the steps which must be followed in its application are the same you won't save any time by using it, but keep it in mind. If you have any furniture around the house that you have been meaning to refinish anyway, by all means get the Zar and do the tackle box with it as well.

Varnish the inside of the box in the same manner to protect it from moisture, and prop the lid open with a small stick while it is drying. For one thing it will dry much faster; for another, if you don't you'll end up with a box stuck solidly together, and you will have to saw it apart and finish it all over again.

Now that the box is drying, we can proceed to the lure trays. While most metal and plastic tackle boxes have cantilever trays, this box will have trays of the stack variety. They are just as effective as the other variety, with the advantages of being completely removable and simple for the average person to make. There is also a certain advantage to the removable trays over the cantilever variety, which by their very action cover the rear portion of the tray immediately beneath them. Anyone who has had the experience of treble-hooked plugs snagging and snarling on the edges of the cantilever trays will recognize the advantage of being able to remove the upper trays completely to gain access to tackle in the lower trays.

The trays themselves are relatively easy to make, except for the divider slots. These take some time. The first step is to cut the 1 × 2-inch boards into ten 6-inch pieces and ten 12-inch pieces. These will be the sides of the trays. The 7½ × 12-inch pieces of ¼-inch plywood will be the bottoms of the trays, but these will not be assembled right at the moment. The next step will be to make the slots for the dividers. If you have access to either a router or a table saw with a dado blade, these will pose no problem, but if you are operating solely with hand tools you will have to cut the slots with a crosscut saw. This is a time-consuming and an exacting process, but luckily you can (in fact, should) do more than one at a time. Take four of the 12-inch sections of 1 × 2 and lay them out on the workbench, 2-inch side up, with the long edges touching. In other words, you will have four sections which will measure an area 6 × 12 inches, because of the actual 1½-inch measure of the 2-inch lumber. The most effective size for compartments in a box of this size is 1½ inches wide. Since the inset 6-inch sides of the trays will take up ¾ inch from each end of the tray, make a mark 2¼ inches from one end of the strips and, with a carpenter's square, mark a line across all the pieces. Move the square ¼ inch further and scribe another line. Move it 1½ inches further and scribe another line; then another ¼ inch move, another 1½ inches, and so on. The compartment on the opposite end of the tray will measure 2 inches in width, plus ¾ inch for the opposite end, allowing a wider compartment for larger lures or tackle. See the diagram for the layout.

Now take a piece of scrap lumber and tack it to the strips so that, when the crosscut saw is laid alongside it, it will cut right along the edge of one of the ¼-inch sections. Holding the saw parallel to the wood, saw back and forth slowly, letting the saw do the work, until you have cut approximately ¼ inch deep into the strips. Now move the saw and the strip of scrap wood so that the saw is against the

Making divider slots with hand saw.

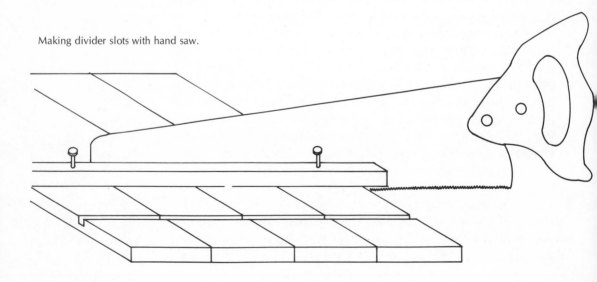

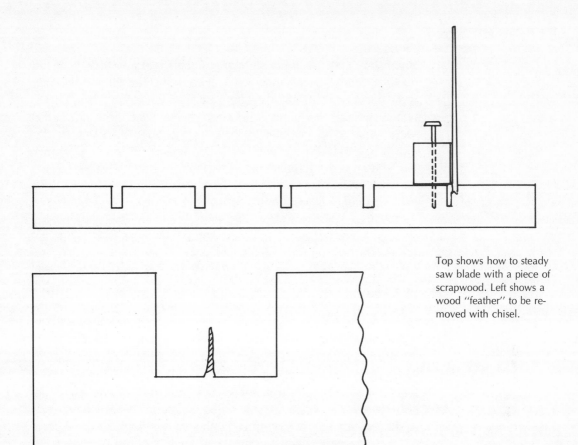

Top shows how to steady saw blade with a piece of scrapwood. Left shows a wood "feather" to be removed with chisel.

other side of the ¼-inch mark. Tack the wood down and proceed to make another cut of the same depth. The normal kerf, or width, of a saw cut is approximately ⅛ inch, so two cuts for each slot should clean out the groove. If you have a saw with an overly thin blade, there will be a "feather" of wood left in the center of the cut. This feather may be pulled loose by the saw, or it can easily be scraped out by working a chisel back and forth in the groove. Proceed to make the other cuts along the four strips in the same manner, and then do the other six strips. I know it sounds like lots of work, but since the slots are only ¼ inch in depth and you are really doing four slots at once, you can turn out all of the divider slots in about 1½ hours. Once you get them done, the rest of the construction is child's play.

After all of the slots are cut, you are ready to assemble the trays. Lay out the 12-inch strips on the 7½ × 12-inch pieces of plywood with the slots facing inward, and make certain that the slots are directly across from one another. Glue the strips down, and fasten through the bottom of the tray with ½-inch brads. Now affix the

6-inch tray ends in the same manner. You will note that with the 1½-inch combined thickness of the two tray sides, the 6-inch ends go in between them with regular butt joints to make a total of 7½ inches, the total width of the plywood sheets. Fasten the ends to the bottom with glue and brads, and fasten the sides of the tray to the ends of the tray with finishing nails. Now sand the tray in the same way you sanded the main box. You won't be able to after the dividers are in. Also, if you wish to stain the trays, do that now as well; use wood filler on them at this point.

Now you are ready for the dividers. Cut the lattice strip into 6½-inch lengths (6 inches for the width of the tray, and ¼ inch to go into each slot). Sand these perfectly smooth, and use wood filler or stain on them. After they are dry, install them in the slots, and give the entire structure several good smooth coats of varnish. This will serve two purposes: it will protect the trays from moisture; and the varnish will seal any small cracks and crevices around the fitting so that hooks won't snag.

One point here: the sizes of the compartments are based upon the most common-sized spinning lures. Should you be using this as a special muskie box, or a box to handle fly boxes, or any other purpose, feel free to adapt the size of the compartments to your special needs. All aspects of constructing the trays would still hold true.

You are now ready to put the finishing touches on the tackle box. Install the trays against one end of the box, one on top of the other. Now take the two 5-inch sections of ¼-inch quarter-round, finish them to fit the rest of the box, and install them with brads ¹/₁₆ inch from the end of the trays. These guides will keep the trays from sliding over into the reel/extra spool/lunch compartment side of the box.

Now, close the box, measure 3 inches in from each end along the open side, and install the two brass catches. On each corner of the box, install one of the brass box corners. These are very important: not only do they add tremendously to the appearance of the box, but also, if the box is accidentally dropped or scraped, the corners are the most likely part to splinter, and the brass corners protect these vulnerable points.

Finally, locate the center of the top of the box, and install the brass door handle. I wish I could be more specific, but brass handles come in different sizes, and different people have different sizes of hands, so you should simply choose the size handle that will be the most comfortable for you. The best way of finding the location is as follows: Measure the length of the handle, and subtract it from 18 inches (the length of the box); divide that by 2 to get the distance in

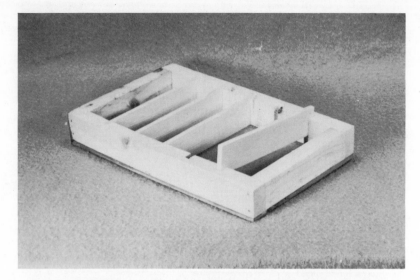

Tray with dividers in place.

Finished spinning box.

from each end, measure in that distance and make a small mark. Then do the same with the width of the handle, subtracting from 9 inches (the width of the box); measure half that distance from each side, and make two marks. Then center the handle on those four marks and screw it down. For example, a 6-inch-long handle 2 inches wide would be installed with its outer edges 6 inches from each end and 3½ inches from each side. You're done!

THE BOAT BOX

Rest assured, this will be a much shorter section than the one on the spinning box. The construction details for the boat box are similar; however, materials and sizes are different, and because plywood is the principal material, the joinery is a little different. This is not a box to carry gaily down the street or to your favorite trout stream. Rather, it is a box designed to remain in your boat, generally in the larger boats designed for deep-water fishing with large lures. Don't expect overwhelming beauty from this one; just a good, functional box that will carry your gear stored properly, and can be easily bolted down at some location in your boat to prevent theft.

BILL OF MATERIALS

2	$\frac{1}{2} \times 10 \times 11''$ marine plywood	ends
2	$\frac{1}{2} \times 10 \times 19''$ marine plywood	sides
2	$\frac{1}{2} \times 12 \times 19''$ marine plywood	top and bottom
5	$\frac{1}{4} \times 11 \times 11''$ tempered Masonite	tray bottoms
10	$\frac{5}{8} \times 2 \times 9\frac{7}{8}''$ marine plywood	tray ends
10	$\frac{5}{8} \times 2 \times 11''$ marine plywood	tray sides
20	$\frac{1}{4} \times 2 \times 10\frac{1}{8}''$ marine plywood	dividers
2	$\frac{1}{2} \times 8''$ quarter-round molding	tray guides
2	3'' brass hinges	
1	large brass door handle	
2	brass catches	
8	large brass box corners	
1	medium brass hasp	
1	small brass padlock	
1	pkg. 1'' brads	
$\frac{1}{2}$ lb.	4d galvanized finishing nails	
	white glue	
	wood filler	
	stain or enamel paint	
	spar varnish	

The procedures to be carried out in making the boat box are exactly the same as in the spinning box, with the following exceptions. The sides are assembled with glue and galvanized finishing nails rather than brass screws, since the end grain of the plywood will not hold a screw too well and will be likely to splinter. As with the spinning box, the sides overlap the ends. However, the top and bottom

The sturdy boat box.

Box stows a lot of tackle.

do not fit inside but instead overlap all the way around. The cut to separate the lid and the bottom should be 2 inches down from the top; and the spacing of the compartments should be a minimum of 2 inches, with a few 3- or 4-inch compartments thrown in for the larger saltwater tackle, bottom rigs, spools of lead core line, and so on.

The box pictured was not constructed with only butt joints; I mitered the joints in front to conceal the raw edges of plywood. If you want to try this method, figure out exactly what the dimensions should be and see if you can get your lumberyard to make the miter cuts.

It would be a good idea to install a hasp and padlock on the center of the front cut. (I hadn't yet done this on the pictured box.) Remember, this box will be living on your boat so that your tackle will be available when you are, and most thieves on boats simply grab and run. If the box is bolted down and the padlock in place, they'll probably only get off with your extra set of clothes.

This box can be painted rather than stained or varnished, because you are never going to turn a box of this size into a work of art. Use epoxy paint—it will resist almost anything.

Well, there you are. You now have either a very attractive, English-type streamside box, or a rather ungainly but eminently durable and practical boat box for saltwater fishing—or both. All you have to do now is load up the box with tackle, get out your favorite rod, and—take the trash out and go fishing.

9
Wooden
Trout Net

All right, so now you have made your custom, British-style wooden tackle box and saved quite a bit of money in the process, and with it sitting at your feet just waiting for the next trip, you're looking at those pictures again. I don't blame you in the least. One of those split bamboo rods is enough to send shivers up the back of any true fly-fisherman. They have the same sort of attraction as those long, willowy models on the covers of some of the fashion magazines.

With most fishermen's pocketbooks today, those rods are, like the models, untouchable. The reels fall into the same category, at least if you want to save a little money for transportation to the stream. So what's left? Well, look at what's hanging at the gillie's hip. Just a trout net? Not on your setter's sainted head! The way that fishing is in the British Isles, anglers there never have "just" anything. There is no bent piece of aluminum tubing for that net frame, no molded rubber grip that's going to dry-rot and flake to pieces. No, that is a genuine wooden-framed net. It isn't a trout net; it's a TROUT NET. And, while this book can't help you with the rod and reel, it can help you to acquire an attractive and functional TROUT NET, similar to the ones which retail for $30 at the time of this writing, for about 75 cents and a few hours' work.

There are, however, certain differences between this net and the professionally manufactured nets of the wooden variety, differences which cannot be practically overcome in the normal home workshop. Professionally made nets are generally of hardwood, often laminated, and the bow of the net is a single piece that has been steamed and bent to shape and fitted to the handle. This sort of net can be made in that manner at home, but the extra equipment needed for the steaming and bending operations—steam tank,

The wooden trout net, homemade.

bending jigs, lamination clamps, and a few other odds and ends—would run the cost of making a single net up to around $60 or $70, and the purpose of this book is not spending money unnecessarily.

BILL OF MATERIALS

1	1 × 8 pine, 12″ long	front of bow
2	1 × 8 pine, 21″ long	sides of bow and handle
4	small brass mending plates	
	brass screws	
1	net bag (purchase, or see Chapter 15 for instructions on how to make)	
½ lb.	small fencing staples	
4′	36-lb.-test braided nylon fishing line	
6″	monofilament fishing line	
	Weldbond glue	
	epoxy cement	
	Duco cement	
3′	#24 nylon cord for attaching net to frame	
1	6 × 2″ pipe nipple for bending the mending plates	
	spar varnish or Zar	

Rather, we will be making a net of softwood—either pine, fir, or spruce. This construction has certain advantages. Once the softwood is properly sealed and finished, the net frame will have excellent buoyancy, and will float readily should you drop it overboard. This buoyancy is of added advantage when landing a fish, since all you have to do is slide the bow under the fish, and let the buoyant wood take care of trapping the fish. Rather than scooping up the catch, all you have to do is slide and lift.

The first step is gluing the stock together for the frame. Glue the boards together as shown in the illustration, and lay out the pattern of the frame as shown. Because the glue joints are critical, and the boards are only butt-jointed together, they should be clamped. If you

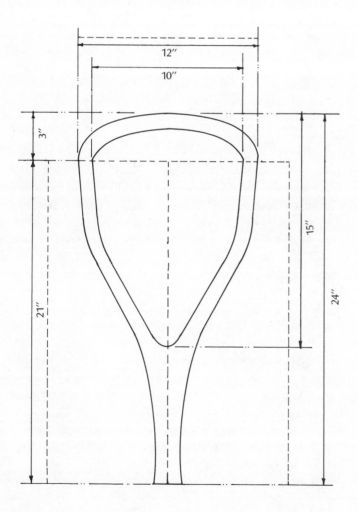

Pattern for trout net frame.

don't have access to bar or pipe clamps that will take care of the distance involved, tie a few loops of rope only slightly larger than the dimensions of the construction, slide them over the boards, insert a large nail or dowel rod (or even a screwdriver) beneath the loop and twist so that it tightens the rope, thus clamping the boards securely. Use a good grade of waterproof glue, such as hide glue or Weldbond, and allow the construction to dry under clamping pressure for 48 hours. Don't take the clamps off sooner. This is a project that cannot be rushed. If you try, all you'll end up with is a net that will fall apart when you are in the middle of landing a 4-pound brown.

Once the glue is thoroughly dry, remove the rope clamps and, using the coping saw, carefully cut out the pattern you have drawn on the wood. The best overall dimensions for a stream net, as shown on the diagram, are 22-inch length and 11-inch width, outside measurements, with a smooth, even taper from the sides of the bow to the handle, and 10×15 inches for the inside measurements of the bow. The bow itself should be $1/2 \times 3/4$ inches thick, with a slight thickening at the top of the bow to strengthen it in case it accidentally knocks against a rock on the stream bottom in shallow water. By gluing the boards together as you did, you make full use of the strength of the wood grain. In other words, they form a frame in which the lines of stress are against the grain of the wood, perpendicular to, rather than parallel with, the flow of the grain.

You might be wondering why the frame could not be made from a single piece of heavy plywood for one-piece, very strong construction. There are two reasons, one practical, one aesthetic. The practical reason is that a plywood frame of this sort, even one made of marine plywood, would eventually warp and separate along the glue lines. The aesthetic reason is that all you would see with a plywood frame would be the plies, and there would be no way of finishing the frame to approach the appearance of the nets we are trying to simulate.

As you can see from the diagram, half of the handle is made with each side of the bow. This provides extra strength. The only point in the net with any inherent weakness will be where the top of the bow joins the sides. To reinforce these joints, take two small brass mending plates, and bend them into a slight curve by hammering them over something round, like a short section of 2-inch-diameter pipe. In fact, you can purchase a 6-inch-long pipe nipple, 2 inches in diameter, for a few nickels. There is no need to purchase a full length of pipe just to bend the brass mending plates.

You will notice that these plates have four holes for screws. Position them so that two of the holes are on the leading edge of the bow

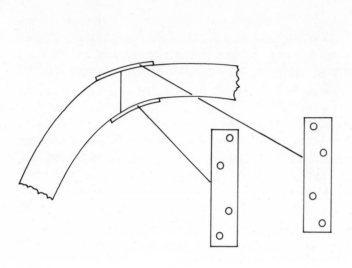

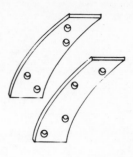

Bend the mending plates to fit the curve of the bow, then glue them in place and fasten with screws. Be sure the screw holes on top do not directly oppose those on the bottom plate.

on either side, and two on the side of the bow. Do this both inside and out (see the illustration for details). Notice that the holes in the mending plates are staggered. Simply reverse the plates so that the holes on the inside of the bow are not directly under the holes on the outside of the bow. If the plates are not reversed, the screws will run into each other when you try to install the plates. Now coat the plates with 2-part epoxy cement and attach to the bow of the net in the proper position. As soon as these are attached with the cement, drill pilot holes and install brass screws through the plates into the wood. Use screws that will reach the opposite side of the wood. The screws are put in after the cement is applied so that the screw threads will carry some of the cement down into the wood, and will bond them strongly. Once these plates have been attached on both sides, the net cannot possibly separate at the joints while you're landing that lunker.

The next step is final shaping and finishing of the net bow. This is really not too difficult, but is best accomplished either with a four-in-one wood rasp or a selection of Surform tools as mentioned in the chapter on hand tools. I prefer a four-in-one wood rasp, not only because it is cheaper, but because there are two different shapes, each in two different degrees of coarseness—flat coarse, flat medium, half-round coarse, and half-round medium—all on the same tool. Rather than laying down one tool and picking up another, all you have to do is turn the wood rasp over or reverse ends to get the exact grit you need for primary shaping.

Now, take the rasp and round every edge, inside and out, taking especial care to smooth and round the handle into a nice taper. The rasp certainly will not finish the job. After you have finished rasping the wood to the rough shape, you must sand down further with progressively finer grits of sandpaper. So don't go hog-wild with the rasp, or you'll end up removing too much stock. After you reach the 220 grit sandpaper, you must install the hanging attachments for the net bag.

Decide which surface of the net bow you want for the bottom of the net (sometimes an interesting grain structure shows up on one side that you might want to show on top), and, laying the net top-down on an old piece of carpet to avoid scratches, drive small fencing staples into the wood at 1¼-inch intervals. Use the smallest fencing staples you can find, and drive them so that only a ¼-inch gap in the staple extends above the surface. Before you do any actual nailing, it would be a good idea to mark the nail locations lightly with a pencil all the way around the frame to make sure they are spaced evenly.

Now turn the net over, and go over all exposed surfaces of the wood, except for the bottom of the bow, with coarse, then medium, and then fine steel wool, to remove all minor dents which may have occurred while installing the staples.

The handle of the net can be finished as is if it has a very attractive grain, but if you put a very smooth finish on the handle, it may become too slippery to hold securely when wet. For this reason, I generally wrap the handle, much like a fishing rod guide.

If you wish to wrap the handle, the procedure is as follows:

Select a good grade of 36-pound-test braided nylon fishing line. A smaller line will still become rather smooth when the net is varnished. A diagram is provided to show the wrapping procedure, which becomes a little confusing in the telling. Choose a color of line that suits you, and cut a 4-foot length. Apply a dab of Duco cement to the net handle, and position one end of the nylon line in the cement as shown in the diagram. After the cement has dried thoroughly, begin wrapping the line around the handle very carefully, making certain that no wood shows through at any point along the handle. Gaps would not affect the efficiency of the wraps, but would certainly affect the appearance. Wrap tightly and smoothly, and allow no overlaps, for 3 inches up the handle. Now take a piece of monofilament line 6 inches long, double it, and lay it over the wraps as shown in the diagram. Continue wrapping the handle for another inch, wrapping over the doubled monofilament, and still keeping the wraps tight and jammed against each other.

After you have finished wrapping that inch, there will be a ¼-inch to ½-inch loop of monofilament extending from beneath the

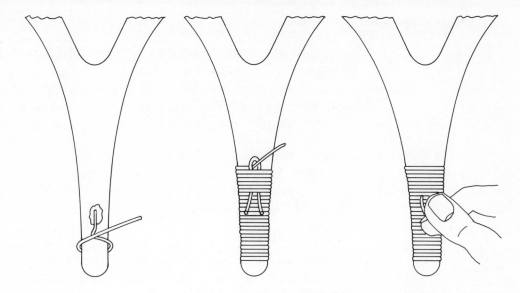

Wrapping the handle. Start with a dab of Duco to anchor the nylon line. The last inch of line should be wrapped over a loop of monofilament, so the end can be secured. The loop works like a needle's eye.

wraps at the bow end of the handle, and two ends trailing from the handle end of the frame. Slip the end of the braided nylon through the loop, holding the end wraps snug, and grasp the trailing ends of the monofilament and pull slowly and steadily. The monofilament will slip through, beneath the wraps, drawing the end of the braided nylon with it. The dab of glue at the beginning of the process and this last little trick buries both ends of the wrapping beneath an inch of the wrap itself, so it cannot unravel. With a razor blade cut the end of the line off flush to the wrappings. The net is ready for final finishing.

There are many excellent products on the market for finishing, and if you paint the net you don't deserve to have it. I recommend either a good grade of spar varnish or exterior Zar, the acrylic coating mentioned in Chapter 8. Whatever you use, use a minimum of three coats, and I strongly recommend five, allowing 24 hours' drying time between each coat. You have already spent a goodly amount of time on this project, and you ought to be very proud of it now, so a few extra days of waiting won't hurt.

In Chapter 15, you will discover how to weave your own nets. I offer both a net bag for this trout net and a nice live bag as examples. Net weaving is fascinating, a marvelous hobby in itself, and quite inexpensive. However, if you are in a hurry to take the net fishing, you can purchase a net bag in most sporting goods stores or through several mail order outlets for less than $1. Whichever you choose to do, after you have the finished bag, lay it out flat and with a stout piece of nylon cord, weave the top meshes of the net to the staples in the frame, making certain that the net doesn't bunch up anywhere along the way.

You may wonder why we didn't simply staple the net to the frame. Well, such a method would have made applying the finish very difficult, and also this frame is permanent. If you use the weaving technique the bag is very easy to replace when it becomes weak or rotten (an extra advantage to making your own nets out of nylon rather than the commercially available cotton or linen, which deteriorate much more rapidly). Knot the nylon cord securely by the handle, cut the ends, and touch each end with a match to prevent fraying.

Time spent making this net is drying time rather than actual working time. But, by now, you see how well worth the wait this net really is. Place it next to your custom wooden tackle box, take a nice proud look—and then go fishing.

10
Fly-Tying Desk

Perhaps one of the greatest problems that fly-tiers face is not the weaving of hair hackles or the creation of an effective flat-bodied nymph imitation, but rather where to store tools and materials and where to do the tying. For the fly-tier who already has storage facilities, the next chapter presents a portable fly-tying bench with a rack for tools and immediately needed materials. It also makes a worthwhile addition to this project, a desk which provides both tying area and storage. This project can be established in one room and the portable bench carried about, say, to the basement or the garage. So consider them both, and build whichever you need.

An actual fly-tying desk, unlike a modification of an existing writing desk, is specifically designed so that its size and height are exactly in keeping with the purpose at hand. Regular desk modifications are far too expensive and the desks themselves are too large. Great depth is not required for fly-tying, and can actually be a disadvantage, as materials may get too far out of hand. Also, if you are as lazy as I am, you will keep piling up materials for different patterns all over the desk until all your materials are on top and you can't find what you need. That is why I developed this fly-tier's desk.

Surprisingly enough, after that list of materials, the desk is actually rather easy to build, and not very expensive. In this project, you will also learn how to build drawers, a technique that will serve you in good stead should you elect to build either the spinner center (Chapter 16), or the gun cabinet (Chapter 30).

The desk, as you can see from both the photograph and the diagrams, is actually built a little like a trestle, with two storage areas, one at either side, and the narrow top joining them to provide a 2-

---

BILL OF MATERIALS

1	1 × 12″ pine, 48″ long	top
1	1 × 8″ pine, 24″ long	rack
4	1 × 10″ pine, 30″ long	sides
2	½ × 12 × 30″ plywood	backs
1	½ × 12 × 24″ plywood	door
1	1 × 8″ pine, 12″ long	bin front
2	1 × 10″ pine, 12″ long	bin bottoms
6	¾ × 9 × 12″ plywood	shelves
8	¼ × 9 × 5″ plywood	drawer sides
4	¼ × 10 × 5″ plywood	drawer backs
4	¼ × 9 × 10″ plywood	drawer bottoms
4	½ × 10 × 5″ plywood	drawer fronts
4	¼ × 12″ pine, 5¼″ long	false drawer fronts
1	¼ × 5″ pine, 12″ long	false bin front
2	1 × 1″ pine, 8′ long	drawer rails
4	drawer pulls	
2	wrought iron hinges	
1	door latch/handle	
	finishing nails	
	brads	
	white glue	
	plastic wood	
	"L" hooks	
3	rubber bands	
Optional:	stain or varnish	
1	#8 round head brass screw	
2	¼″ brass washers	
2	¼″ hole, ¾″ diameter rubber washers	

foot-wide kneehole. The first step, therefore, is to build the two storage areas. After they are built, the rest is simple.

Lay out the pieces designated as sides, backs, bottoms, door, bin front, false bin front, and rails. Assemble the backs to the sides, with the backs sitting inside of the side pieces, with simple butt joints. All assembly is done with white glue and finishing nails. Now install the bin bottoms between the sides and back, and flush with the floor. Attach both the real and the false bin fronts to the fronts of the two sections, so that the lower edge contacts the bin bottom.

Up to this point, all construction methods have been the same for both storage sections. Now we will diversify, making one of the

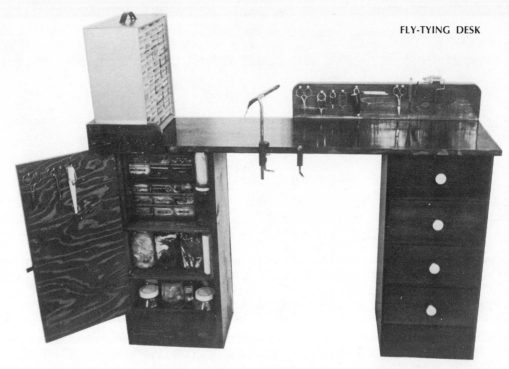

A fly-tying desk will give you an organized work and storage space.

sections into a drawer storage area and the other into a shelf-and-bin storage area.

Take the section with the real bin front mounted at its bottom, and install the door piece with two hinges, one of them 6 inches down from the top, the other 6 inches up from the bottom. Install the friction catch, following the directions printed on the packaging, and then install the door handle.

Now take the pieces designated as shelves and mount them inside the section with white glue and finishing nails driven through the sides and back. I am not going to give height positions for the shelves,—you are the best judge of the shelf positions that suit your personal needs. I have mine arranged so that at least one shelf contains the fly-tying manuals that I use most frequently; that way I leave the bench only for a special pattern in a special book that I want to try as an experiment. The bin at the bottom of this section is designed to hold large and bulky material like bucktails. If you wish, the shelves can be positioned so that small plastic drawer cabinets (the kind used in workshops to hold nails and screws) can be installed to hold small pieces of fur, floss, chenille, hooks, and so on.

Now we are ready for the drawer section. The rails are positioned 6 inches apart on center—that is, starting 5½ inches above the

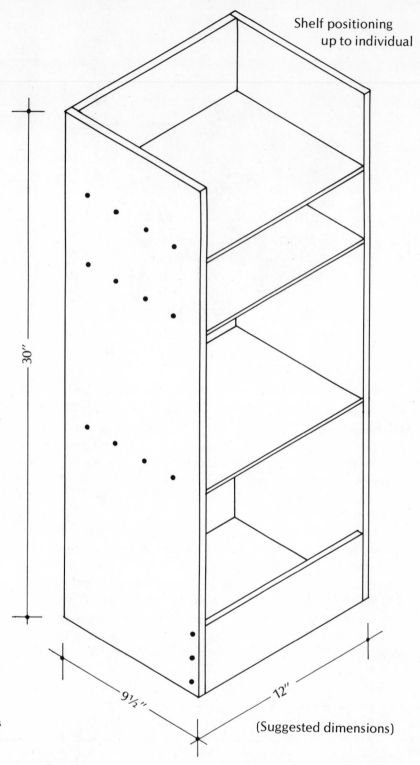

Shelf positioning
up to individual

30"

9½"

12"

(Suggested dimensions)

Shelf cabinet with shelves
and bin installed. Shelves
are secured by nails, as
shown.

66

bottom, then 11½ inches above the bottom, 17½ inches above the bottom, and 23½ inches above the bottom. These are glued into position and attached with finishing nails.

It's time to build the drawers. There are many ways of fitting the drawers together, from tongue and groove through slotted inlay to dovetail joints. If you are familiar with any of these processes, feel free to use them. Otherwise, use simple butt joints, attaching them with white glue and brads.

The simplest way of assembling the drawers is to lay out the drawer bottoms, apply glue along the front and rear edges (the 10-inch sides), fit the front and rear sections up against them, and attach with the brads. With glue, coat the side edges of the drawer bottom, as well as the side edges of the front and back, and attach the

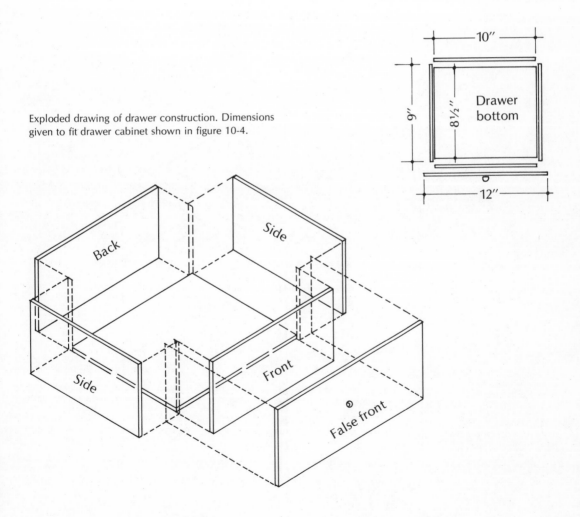

Exploded drawing of drawer construction. Dimensions given to fit drawer cabinet shown in figure 10-4.

sides with brads. You will notice from the instructions and the diagram that the front and rear of the drawers fit inside the sides, and the bottom fits inside all the other pieces. That way, the brads enter the drawer bottom parallel with the plane of the bottom, and give extra support to any weight placed in the drawers.

Now center the actual front of the drawer on the piece marked false front, 1 inch from either side, ¼ inch from the top, and flush

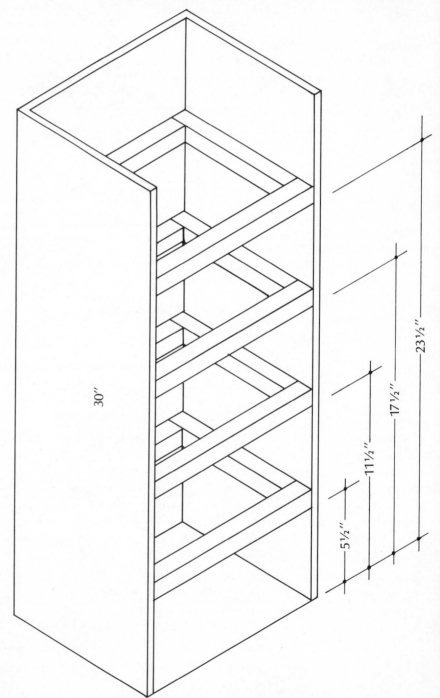

Drawer cabinet with drawer rails installed.

with the bottom of the drawer. Mark a line around the piece using the actual front of the drawer as a guide, coat the front of the drawer with glue, and attach with brads. Now find the dead center of the *false* front by connecting opposite corners of the false front with light pencil lines. Drill a hole at the intersection of these lines, and install the drawer pull. Proceed with all the drawers in this manner, and then slide them into the storage section along the rails.

You will find that there will be a slight gap at the top of the section, and because of differences in saw kerfs and other construction procedures, this gap will vary from desk to desk. For this reason, I have not given overall dimensions for the single top rail that will fill this gap. Measure carefully, cut a piece of scrap lumber to fit, and install it between the sides. Now the lips of the drawers formed by the false fronts will overlap the rails, allowing for a better seal, and preventing the drawers from sliding too far into the storage area.

You're coming down the home stretch now. Attach the top piece to the upper edges of the two storage sections so that the rear edge of the top is flush with the rear of the storage sections and the ends are flush with the outer edges of the sections. This construction will leave an overlap at the front and provide a 2-foot-wide kneehole between the sections. Attach the top with glue and finishing nails as you did for all the other joints. Now attach the rack to the rear edge of the top so that it extends above the top of the desk. The half-width rack eliminates wasted space, and can be located for right-hand or left-hand convenience. If you desire, you can trim the upper corners of the rack round with a coping saw. Although this step isn't necessary, it looks better and prevents snagging your arm on the corner should you happen to bump into it.

Now take a countersink (nail punch) and go over the desk, sinking every nail used in the construction approximately ⅛ inch below the surface of the wood, and fill all the resulting holes with plastic wood. Allow this to dry thoroughly, and then sand the entire desk smooth, starting with an 80 grit paper and proceeding to 220 grit. If you have done it properly, you shouldn't be able to tell where the nail went in. Now stain the desk, and apply two or three coats of varnish or Zar. A fly-tier's desk tends to get scratched, and I have found that the acrylic coating resists scratching better than varnish. In addition, many of the cements and solvents used in fly-tying can be wiped or rubbed off the acrylic surface without discoloring or dissolving the finish.

Once the finish has dried completely, take the small "L" hooks, or cup hooks, and install them in the rack, positioning them to hold your tools—two hooks for scissors, one for whip finisher, one for hackle pliers, and so on. At one end of the rack, place a few hooks 4 inches apart, with the hook parallel to the bench top, and stretch small rubber bands between them. These will hold the most-often-used hackle necks while you are working.

That is the basic construction of the fly-tier's desk; however, certain options can make the desk more effective for your own purposes. I will offer a few here, and you can go on from there.

The optional parts list in the bill of materials assumes that you do not already have a thread clip. You can make one that is permanently attached to the desk. Mount your vise, and move it about until you find the most comfortable position. Then drill a small pilot hole into the front edge of the bench, 6 inches to the right of the vise column (to the left if you're left-handed). Take the brass wood screw, and drop on one brass washer, then the two rubber washers, and finally the second brass washer. Now turn the screw snugly into the pilot hole so that the two rubber washers are in contact with each other but not jammed too tightly. Then, when you are tying flies, simply bring the tying thread over and catch it between the rubber washers. They will hold it firmly without fraying or cutting it, and it is a simple matter, once you get used to it, to put the thread in and take it out without even looking.

1¼″ holes for film cans

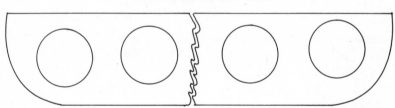

Options for fly-tying desk include film can rack for inside of door (top) and thread holder.

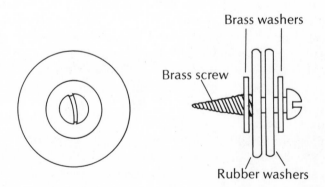

Brass washers

Brass screw

Rubber washers

Another option involves the door to the shelf storage area. If you like, you can install hooks on the inside of the door, positioning them between the shelves, to hold extra tools such as heavy-duty scissors, extra hackle pliers, and so on, rather than having them all on the upper rack. During the construction of the desk, you can also fit strips of wood on the rear side of the door, again positioning them so that they won't run into the shelves. Make these strips of regular 1-inch (nominal) pine, 2 inches wide and 9 inches long, and drill 1¼-inch holes through them to hold film cans containing your hooks, just as you did for the streamside fly-tying kit.

Well, that's about it. We fly-tiers are inventive, and know our own personal needs, so feel free to make any minor additions and modifications that you feel will be of advantage. Now take a look at the portable fly-tying bench in the next chapter, and see if you can't find some use for that elsewhere in your house.

11
Portable Fly-Tying Bench

The portable fly-tying bench is of great advantage on those days when you simple can't spend time wherever the desk is, or if you don't have room for the desk and your wife objects to your clamping the vise and thread clip to the dining room table.

The portable bench can be carried from room to room, and provides no storage area whatsoever—just a place to mount the vise and thread clip, to hang the most useful tools, and to stick a few of the immediately necessary materials while actually in the process of tying. It is designed also to be convenient and small enough to store in a closet until needed. The base is lined to not scratch furniture.

BILL OF MATERIALS

1	1 × 12" pine, 18" long	base
2	1 × 2" pine, 5" long	supports
1	1 × 3" pine, 11½" long	shelf
2	1 × 2" pine, 4" long	rack ends
2	¼ × 4 × 15" plywood	rack sides
1	11½ × 18" felt	base padding
2	film cans	
	finishing nails	
	white glue	
	plastic wood	
	brads	
	cup hooks	
	stain and varnish	

The construction is eminently simple and the cost is extremely low. In fact, the project can be finished in a single evening, and, after the stain and varnish dry, be ready to use the next night.

Construction is quite simple. Use glue and 6d finishing nails for the construction, countersinking all nails and filling with plastic wood before finishing.

The illustration shows clearly how the portable bench is constructed.

Nail the supports to the base, aligning them with the base so that they are flush against one end and the sides as shown. Coat the bottoms of the supports with glue, put them into position with the base upside-down on top of them, and drive the nails through the bottom of the base. Use two nails for each support, and countersink them well.

Now turn the bench back over so that the base is resting on your work bench, apply glue to the upper ends of the supports, and nail the vise shelf to the top of the supports. There will be a 1-inch overlap, which should extend out past the end of the base.

Construct the rack separately. Apply glue along the edges of the rack ends, and, using brads, nail the plywood sides to the ends. Turn the bench over again and, applying glue to the bottom edges of the rack, install it along the rear edge of the base. The vise shelf should be located on the left for right-handers, on the right for southpaws.

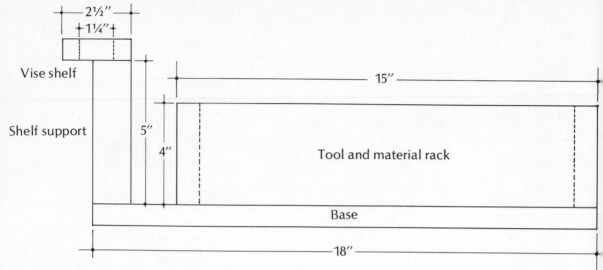

Frontal view of portable fly-tying bench.

Now sand the entire construction thoroughly, except for the vise shelf, taking special care to get the exposed ends and edges of plywood as smooth as possible. Most plywood has gaps along the edges. Fill those gaps with plastic wood and allow it to dry thoroughly before sanding. Once the bench has been finished, it will give the appearance of solid wood, unless the edges are closely examined.

Before you sand the vise shelf, take a 1¼-inch drill bit and bore two holes, through the top toward the rear of the bench and centered on the width of the shelf, as shown in figure 3. These holes will hold two film cans containing hooks. Now sand the vise shelf as smooth as the rest of the bench, and go over the whole construction with steel wool to give the wood a gloss.

Turn the construction over again, coat the entire bottom with white glue, and apply the piece of felt. Smooth it out, working out all wrinkles and air pockets, using either your fingers, a straightedge, or, even better, a good rolling pin.

Finally, apply a good stain and two or three coats of varnish and allow to dry. Install cup hooks in the front of the rack to hold one pair of scissors, a pair of hackle pliers, a bodkin, and whatever other tools are used constantly in your work. Install the film cans for the hooks, mount your vise, and you're ready to tie.

Incidentally, a thread holder can be installed on the inner edge of the vise shelf. Simply follow the directions for the construction of the thread holder given in the preceding chapter.

This bench is excellent for moving around the house, or for leaving in a vacation cabin, but it is a little too bulky for normal travel. If you must tie flies when you travel, I strongly recommend the streamside fly-tying kit in Chapter 5. It is much more compact, and although you won't be able to tie the larger saltwater flies with the midge vise, you will be able to "match the hatch" in Nos. 8 to 24. If you have built the streamside kit, the fly-tier's desk, and the portable bench and still have trouble finding a place to whip up a dozen March Browns, you're just out of my league.

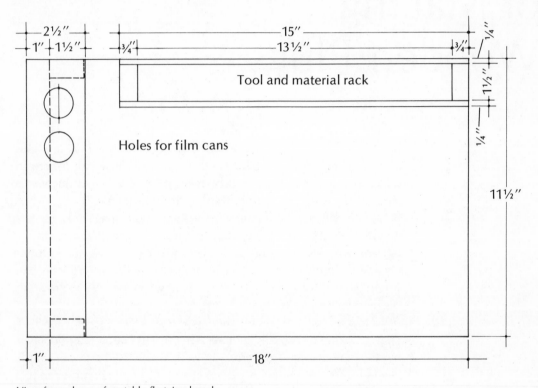

View from above of portable fly-tying bench.

12

The Art
of Making
Wooden Plugs

With the tremendous body of material in both magazines and books written for the fly-tier, it has long seemed to me that the plug fisherman has gotten the short end of the stick. Live-bait fishermen shake their heads at him; fly-fishermen mutter under their breaths at him. While expert plug fishermen write tomes about how to fish a plug, you will never see one of the leading sports magazines running an article on the latest killing plug and how to make it. Rather, they'll tell you what it is, and perhaps where you can buy it. And with the cheapest plastic plugs coming in at between $2 and $5, the plug fisherman is more or less a homeless waif when it comes to providing his own tackle at a reasonable sum.

Now, many companies, such as Herter's, Finnysports, and Netcraft, to name a few, sell compression-formed plastic plug-bodies in most of the standard patterns, as well as all the hardware that is needed. They are so easy to put together that a babe-in-arms can turn out an excellent plastic plug and finish it in 10 minutes, and yet I have seen some books which devote half a chapter to telling the sportsman how to glue the bloody things together. Granted, these bodies are an excellent value over the commercially manufactured plugs, but I'll tell you a secret: modern progress and advertising claims be damned, I *hate* plastic plug bodies. And to make matters worse, I grew up with them.

However, when I was in my teens, I ran across an old tackle box in a junk shop, and in it were five weatherbeaten, fish-chewed plugs from the early days of manufacture, all built by the Heddon Company, and all made of wood and finely lacquered. I stared at them, felt the solidity of them, bought the whole lot for $2, and I was hooked for life. Over the next few years I fished with them, and the action was far superior to any of the plastic products I had been using, even the ones which were supposed to be exact replicas of the wooden ones I had. But when I lost two of them to muskies, I retired the rest to a glass case.

Those old plugs are genuine antiques, and over the past 15 years I have only located two that people have been willing to sell. But, because of the superiority of the wooden plug for fishing, I began making my own. You can, too, and it really isn't difficult at all. In fact, I don't even believe that this is the sort of thing that you could call a project. More likely it is something to do in an overstuffed chair in front of a fire on a rainy day in December or January, while your mind is off somewhere on your favorite bass lake tied into a 15-pound largemouth on 4-pound-test monofilament.

You can experiment with plugs by purchasing the smallest screw eyes obtainable at your local hardware store, but I can't really recommend it. First, they are more expensive than necessary; second, they are generally made out of a material that will rust quite easily, especially if used in salt water; third, even the smallest of them are too large for any except lunker-sized or saltwater plugs. Rather, purchase the hardware from any of the catalog houses that offer it. These pieces are usually made of nickel or chrome-plated brass, or even stainless steel, and can be purchased proportioned to the smallest effective plug you would want to make.

A collection of old factory-made wood plugs.

At the time of writing, the various components are quite inexpensive in quantity, with screw eyes costing from 79 cents to $1.17 for a full gross; wiggle plates in the neighborhood of 50 cents a dozen; plug propellers for the injured minnow types which are so effective on early season bass about 40 cents a dozen; nose washers about 10 cents a dozen; and hook hangers at less than 20 cents a dozen. The hardware is so inexpensive and so good that it really doesn't pay to try to economize on it. It is false economy, and the results won't be as good. For an investment of about $3 or $4, including hooks, you can equip about 50 plugs or so, and that isn't bad, even if you are experimenting with a new style rather than copying a proven killer.

Far and away the best wood for plug bodies is cedar: it is a relatively light wood, fairly easy to carve, and has excellent characteristics in the water. In addition, it holds the various fasteners, even the tiny screws that are used to affix the wiggle plates and hook hangers. You may also use pine and other woods (some of the best saltwater plugs I have ever used on giant stripers were hand-carved of teak by the captain of the charterboat). Naturally, the harder woods are more difficult to shape with hand tools. Although a lathe will turn out excellent plugs in one-tenth the time, one can hardly justify an expense of over $100 for a tool just to make plug bodies, unless you are going to make them to sell.

I advise against using balsa wood—it is *too* soft. It will not hold hook hangers and screw eyes, and it won't stand up to the beating that big fish will give it. I know that the rapala type of plug makes a great success out of being made from balsa, but it uses a through-wire construction. Fish like blues and members of the pike family tear those balsa minnows to shreds after half-a-dozen strikes.

I will explain the through-wire construction in this chapter, because any plug will take a beating and perhaps break under the onslaught of a school of blues, and to have the fish still connected to the line by a length of wire when the plug body gives way is a decided advantage. If you want to mess around with balsa, go ahead and do it, but don't expect the plugs to stand up anywhere near as long as ones made of stouter material.

Plug bodies for the most part are round, and this roundness from most of the stock you will be using is achieved by carving. Other writers may tell you to do this with a pocket knife—don't fall for it. I will admit that I have seen some men carve plugs and models of birds and animals using only a pocket knife, and their animal carvings are so realistic you expect them to walk away. That's fine. I have also seen men who have killed bears, both black and grizzly, with a .22

revolver. That's also fine, but I for one don't have the skill to do either one. Carving itself is not difficult, but you need the proper tools if you're just a beginner. In the case of plugs this means a set of hobby knives such as those that go under the brand name "X-acto." These have replaceable blades, and you can get by with one handle and an assortment of blades of different shapes. They are sharp as a razor, so be careful; used properly, they will shave down wood precisely and easily, and make the rounding of the stock a very simple, if time-consuming, matter.

You may also think of using dowels for your plugs. Certainly this eliminates much of the hard work of rounding the stock, but there is one point to bear in mind. Dowels are generally made of hardwood, and the carving of details and the tapering of the plugs to shape is going to be more difficult than when working with pine or cedar. It's just another case of "Ya pays yer money and ya takes yer choice."

There is another alternative, which adds to the cost of the plugs but does save time. Many of the better lumberyards have lathes on hand, and would be willing, for a small charge, to turn a few lengths of pine or cedar into long cylinders for you. In this manner you could have dowels made out of the proper wood for carving. It all depends upon whether or not your time is worth more to you than the cost of having the wood turned. But whatever you do, keep a few square or rectangular blocks on hand, since there will probably be some shapes you will wish to carve that have flats on them, and there would be less carving involved in those cases than if you had to flatten the sides of dowels.

The diagram shows several different standard plug styles, but don't consider yourself limited to these. You can duplicate any plug style in existence with the use of a little tool called a contour gauge, which is generally used by carpenters for duplicating decorative moldings. It consists of a shaft that holds a line of long steel pins, which slide through the shaft. When one side of the gauge is pressed against an irregular surface, the pins move, but since they are friction-tight, when the gauge is removed they retain the shape of the object to be duplicated. This outline can then be transferred to the wood by tracing it with a pencil.

On the other hand, if you have an idea for a plug that you feel ought to beat the professionals, make some sketches and then try carving it. Whatever method you use, make representations of the plug as seen both from the side and the top. As you carve, you will undoubtedly carve away the lines that you have drawn on the piece of wood as guidelines, so you may have to draw them over again a number of times. Make a paper or cardboard template which can be

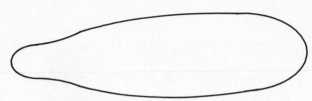

PLOPPER STYLE
Topwater plug, dished in face.

MINNOW
Can be used as quiet topwater plug, or
with wiggling lip as shallow runner.

RUNT STYLE
Used with wiggling lip for shallow,
subsurface running, or bored and
weighted with split shot, plus wiggling
lip, for deep running.

DARTER STYLE
Shallow runner. The notched "mouth"
eliminates the need for the metal lip.

TORPEDO STYLE
This variety is generally used as a
topwater plug with propeller-type
spinner both fore and aft.

PIKE MINNOW
Almost always used with metal lip as
shown. This sort of lip can be home
made from a flattened can.

Six easily made plug bodies.

used to trace the lines on the wood as many times as necessary. Save these templates, especially if you find that the plug is effective or you happen to like the pattern very much. This saves having to duplicate the contouring and the tracing each time you want to make a plug of that pattern. Should you find a plug that is a real killer, laminate the template with those little plastic kits that come in vending machines and most stationery stores for laminating driver's licences. That way the pattern will last for many years, and save you quite a bit of trouble.

After the initial carving the plug will be rather rough. Leave the carving in its rougher stages a little larger than the proposed dimensions of the finished product, since each additional finishing operation will remove a bit more wood. Smooth it down with a rasp and sandpaper. When the plug is as smooth as you can get it with sandpaper, and reduced to its proper dimensions, soak it for an hour in warm water to raise the grain, let it dry overnight, and remove the whiskers of the grain with steel wool. You are now ready to apply the finish.

There are several ways of applying finish to the plugs. Many plug makers use aerosol cans of spray paint. These certainly are handy and come in a variety of colors. There are, however, certain disadvantages which should be considered. Spray paint is not going to hit only the plug; it goes around it and past it as well. If you are going to keep your house or shop from looking like an LSD trip you will have to build a spray box. This isn't really difficult. Just take an old cardboard box, about the size of a whiskey case, and remove the flaps.

The best way of making the spraying box effective is to attach a 6-inch length of wire to one side of the box by threading it through and tying it to a short length of wood on the outside. Now attach a snap swivel to the end inside the box. At the opposite end of the box, punch a ¼-inch hole, and shove a length of dowel through. The length of the dowel will be determined by the distance between that side of the box and the end of the snap swivel. Add 3 inches to that length, cut off the dowel, and install an open-end screw eye in the end of the dowel which is inside the box.

When you get ready to spray the plug body, attach a screw eye to both the nose end and the tail end of the plug, attach one of these eyes to the snap swivel, hook the open-end screw eye on the dowel through the other screw eye in the plug, and draw the dowel back until the plug is suspended rigidly in the center of the box. Take your spray can and have at it, turning the dowel with one hand as you do. This will rotate the plug on the snap swivel so that all sides can be

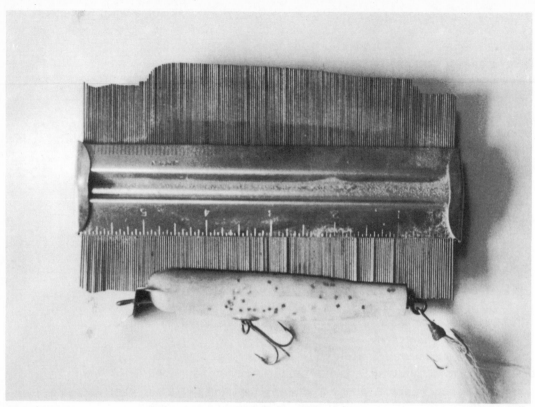

The shape of a plug can be reproduced with a contour gauge.

Trace the shape taken by the gauge on a block of wood.

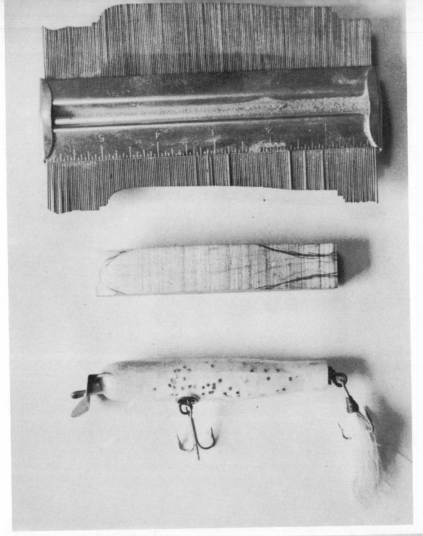

Which is cut to a crude shape with a crosscut saw. . . .

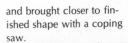

and brought closer to finished shape with a coping saw.

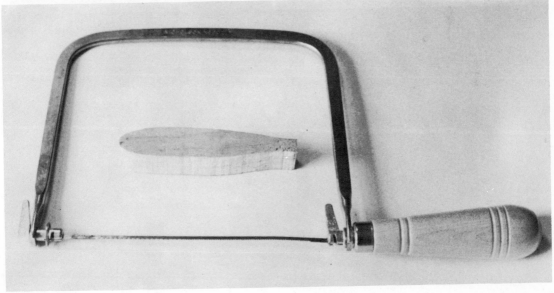

The block shape is rounded
off with a whittling knife.

Smooth the plug with rasp
and sandpaper.

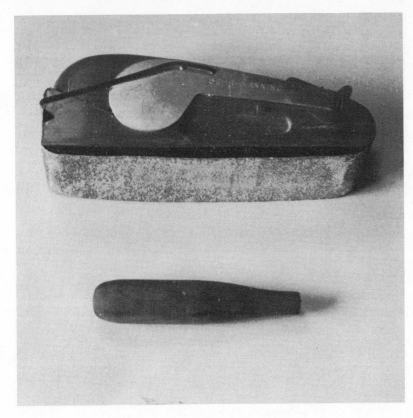

After soaking, drying and smoothing with steel wool, the plug is ready to be finished.

covered without touching the plug. Use several light coats rather than one heavy one to avoid drips and runs.

Currently on the market are some epoxy spray enamels which are used for painting or touching up appliances. These make an exceptionally hard finish that will stand up to quite a bit of abuse.

The plug can also be finished by dipping it into either enamel or lacquer. Put a screw eye in the nose, but not all the way, so that a section of the shank of the eye sticks out. Then dip the plug, and hang it on a wire over a thick pad of newspapers to drain. Whether you use lacquer or enamel, make the paint as thin as possible while still retaining good color coverage, so that the excess paint will run off readily. Otherwise you will end up with lumps, drips, and streaks, which not only look like hell but also destroy the balance of the plug in the water.

There are many ways to dress up a plug once the major color has been applied. There are various appliqués, such as decal eyes and decal scale finish; you can use tape to mask off certain areas and then spray again with a different color; or you can use a fine artist's brush to paint in details. You can also obtain a scale finish netting, used in conjunction with the spray box and spray paint. In use, the plug is usually painted a dark color, and the spray netting is held in a

Here are 10 plugs made by Loring Wilson. Note the variety of shapes.

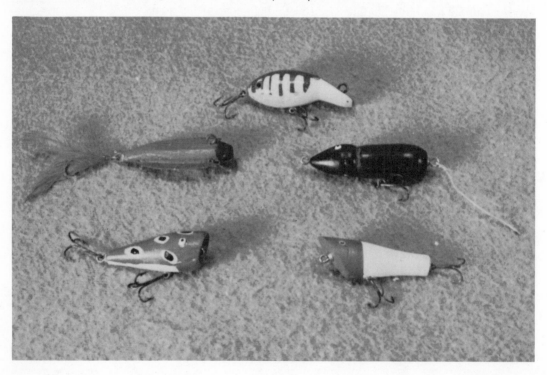

frame. The plug is then held against the netting, and a fast-drying silver spray lacquer or enamel is sprayed through the netting onto the plug, very lightly so that there are no runs. This is tricky, and I honestly question its effectiveness; I tend to believe that plugs with scale finishes are designed more to catch the fisherman's eye than that of the fish. When a fish attacks a plug he is going on the general shape, the general coloration, and, most important, the action of the plug in the water. The scales may make the plug look more like a fish to us, but how can we explain the tremendous number of fish caught on red-and-white, yellow, orange, black, and fluorescent pink plugs? However, the decorations are up to you, and since psychology has a great deal to do with fishing, if you really believe that a scale finish makes your plugs more effective, by all means use it. If you have more confidence in your lures you'll fish them better, and so you'll catch more fish.

Now the plug is carved to shape and painted, so now it's time to install the hardware. Before we get into the installation of the conventional hardware, I want to explain the through-wire construction for use with both balsa plugs and with conventional wooden bodies designed for luring large, toothy fish. The through-wire construction involves running a length of heavy stainless-steel wire through the body of the plug, and attaching the hooks to that wire. The end of the wire

After painting, install the hardware.

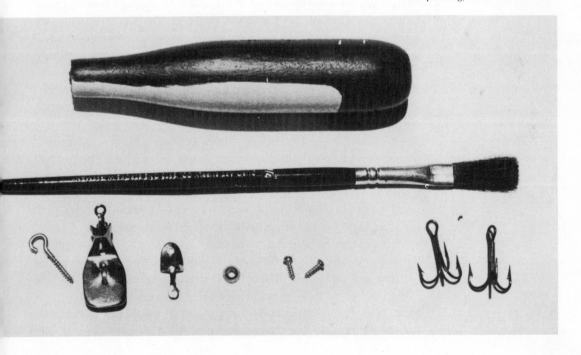

protruding from the nose of the plug is then either formed into an eye itself, or attached to a swivel and then the line. That way, even if the fish completely destroys the body of the plug, as long as he is solidly hooked he will remain hooked.

There are two basic methods of making the through-wire construction. One involves a considerable amount of precision; the other involves a bit more physical work. Both have their own advantages under given circumstances.

The first method, which involves precision work, depends upon drilling two holes. That doesn't sound so bad, but the first hole has to go precisely through the center of the plug the long way, from the center of the nose to the center of the tail, and the second has to come through the belly of the plug and exactly intersect the lengthwise hole. Without a drill press and a series of clamps this is extremely difficult to do, but it can be used on the dowels or already-round stock, and on fully carved plugs. However, should you make a mistake the plug will be unusable, and all the carving you have done will have gone to waste.

The second method is more surefire, even though it requires more work. In this method, the plug is made in two halves from flat stock. Find the center line of each section and cut a groove with the saw down that center line the same as you did with the trays for the wooden tackle box. Now, with one of the hobby knives, make a V-shaped groove from the center slot to one edge of the wood, approximately one-third of the way from one end. Do the same with the other piece so that when the two halves are put together the grooves will coincide. (See figure 10.) You don't have to make them deep, since each groove forms half of the final groove. Glue the two halves together, making certain that both grooves line up with their mates, and that you don't get any glue in the slots. Clamp them together, and leave them overnight.

Certainly this method takes longer, but you can make up a batch in advance so they'll be ready when you want to carve. The method has the added advantage of making certain that the holes are centered in the wood, so you can taper the plug body to the holes instead of drilling the holes through the taper. I prefer this method, since it doesn't waste the plugs I have already shaped.

Regardless of how the holes are made, the means of attaching the wire and hooks is the same. Take a length of 30-pound-test braided steel wire, nylon-coated, and shove one end through the hole in the nose of the plug, almost to the point where the other hole intersects. Now take a small barrel swivel and shove it up into the belly hole of the plug so that the upper eye is in the longitudinal slot, and

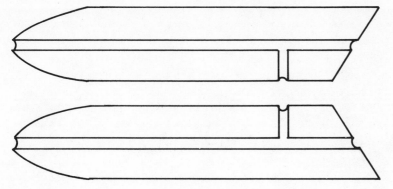

Plug body made from two flat sections. Two sections are then cemented together.

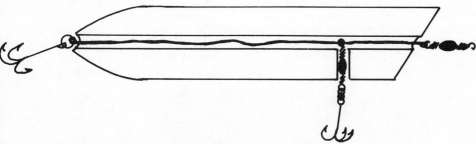

Cross section of assembled plugs, showing method by which hardware is attached to wire.

push the wire on through so that it passes through the eye of the swivel and out the tail of the plug. Form an eye at the tail, either by crimping or wrapping, and attach a split ring to the eye thus formed. Now pull the wire forward so the split ring fits lightly against the tail of the plug. Coat a nose washer with a little Duco cement and slip it over the wire and up against the nose of the plug. Then form an eye at the nose of the plug, as close to the plug as is humanly possible. Attach a split ring to the swivel sticking out of the plug's belly, and put on your hooks, either single or treble, depending upon your preference. That's it. As I have said, these plugs are primarily for the large, toothy fish such as lunker pike and muskies, and for many of the saltwater species. For bass and walleyes, the fish for which most plugs are probably used, they simply aren't necessary. Use the conventional style of hook attachments.

The conventional hook attachments are simple to install, but in the case of the screw eyes it is advisable to drill small pilot holes to

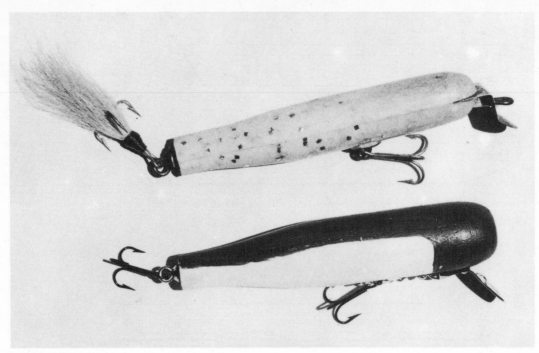

Finished through-wire plugs.

avoid wringing the eye off the soft plated-brass shaft while turning the eye into the wood. A screw starter is also a good substitute for a pilot hole. At any rate, since the eyes are small, the hole should be no larger than 1/16 inch, and no longer than two-thirds the length of the shaft.

It is also advantageous to apply nose washers at the base of the screw eyes, especially on the tail and nose eyes. Hook hangers, at least in my opinion, are better than screw eyes for the belly hook(s). My experience has been that a fish in the water has greater leverage against the belly screw eye than he does against the tail hook, because the plug will turn more easily in the water if he is hooked at the tail hook. The hook hanger, attached by two screws, cannot twist out.

Depending upon the characteristics of the individual plug, you may wish to add wiggle plates to make the plug run under water, or propellers to make a ruckus on the surface as in injured minnow plugs. If you use the propellers, use a longer screw eye and slip a bead on each side of each propeller before installation. The beads will provide a bearing for the propeller, and keep it from hanging up on the nose of the plug or the tail hook.

Making your own plugs is fun and relaxing, and it gives the plug-fisherman the same sort of satisfaction that the fly-fisherman gets when he captures a wily fish on a lure he has created himself; especially if it is a new development not available in the stores. So get some wood and some hardware and have at it. Who knows? You may come up with a pattern so effective it might be purchased by one of the leading manufacturers, and you'll be set for life. Just think of all the extra fishing time you'll get in.

13
Trolling
Speed
Indicator

Prospecting for fish by trolling is one of the most effective means of locating a school, and, in the case of lake trout, it is sometimes the best way of catching them as well. Saltwater fishermen troll because they must find fish on the great blue expanses. But fish swimming at a certain depth won't rise or sink to a lure passing over their heads or too far beneath them.

Many attempts at standardizing depths have been made; the color-coded trolling line is perhaps the most famous. If you meet a school of fish with 100 yards of line out, you can easily locate them again by letting out the line until the color shows you have 100 yards out. Right? Wrong. If you troll with the wind and your speed is two

Despite its modest appearance, this trolling speed indicator really does the job.

knots, when you swing back into the wind your speed will be reduced, even though you keep your motor turning up the same revolutions. Water speed is what is important, and that is what the trolling speed indicator measures.

This project has nothing to build, and it can be done in about ten minutes. But more important, it really works. There is only one thing to purchase if you don't already have one, and that is a fisherman's scale. An inexpensive one which goes to about 30 pounds can be had for about $2. I wouldn't trust that model for weighing fish; but the calibrations for weight are not an issue in this project. What is needed is the hook connected to a needle on a pressure spring, and the cheap scale is the easiest way to get it.

	BILL OF MATERIALS	
1	fish-weighing scale	speed gauge
1	1-lb. coffee can	resistance
3	large snap swivels	connectors
2'	braided wire	bridle
25'	Monel	

When you have the scale, make five or six evenly spaced and easily seen marks along the scale calibrations. Now, take a standard one-pound coffee can, and punch a hole just beneath the rim on either side of the can. If the can has a resealable plastic lid, save it.

The only other materials you will need are three large snap swivels, a 2-foot length of braided, heavy copper wire, and 25 feet of Monel. Braided wire is limper and does not tend to kink and break as solid wire does. Use copper so that it will not rust or corrode.

Take 2 feet of the wire, and attach one of the snap swivels to each end. Twist a loop in the center, and hook the snap swivels into the holes you punched in the can.

Now take a 25-foot length of Monel and tie it firmly to the loop in the center of the 2-foot section of braided wire. At the other end, attach the third snap swivel. Take a pair of pliers, close the hook in the scale so that it makes a tight loop, and snap the long piece of wire onto that loop.

Now all that remains is to affix the indicator to the boat. A screw hook on the transom to hook into the handle of the scale works fine. To use, drop the coffee can overboard, and let it fill with water.

When the boat is in motion, the resistance created by the drag of the can in the water will pull the can backwards, thus moving the needle along the scale. The marks you made tell you how much drag is present. With the one-pound can at trolling speeds, there won't be too much pressure for the scale, but for heaven's sake pull the thing in before you speed up to go somewhere else.

How does it work? Say that you are trolling with the wind, and the needle on the scale is on the third mark when you catch the first fish. So you swing the boat around at the end of the pass, let out the same amount of line, and head back into the wind. But the wind slows the boat down so that the needle is midway between the second and third line. Watching the needle, slowly increase the motor speed until the needle moves back to its original position. Your lure will be at the same depth at which you caught the first fish.

I mentioned saving the plastic lid. At the end of the fishing trip, unhook all the wires and the scale, place them all in the can, and snap the lid on. They will be protected, and you won't be tripping over them. There is only one further point: be careful not to turn the boat sharply across the line, or it will get tangled in the propeller.

14
Bug Cutter

No, this chapter doesn't refer to the Jack the Ripper of the insect world. This is a little gadget for the man who makes his own cork-bodied popping bugs. These effective little critters can be used for almost every type of fish, but they are time-consuming to make as they require that the face of the bug be cut at an angle, and that a thin slot be cut along the bottom of the cork, perfectly aligned with the face, to serve as anchorage for the hook. Since these lures are lightweight fly-rod lures, and have a high mortality rate, the bug fisherman usually needs quite a few, and to make them in the conventional manner with a razor blade is not only slow and tedious, but also dangerous if the razor blade should slip. Also, doing the slot and face by hand often causes problems with alignment. The bug cutter makes both cuts precisely and at the same time, so that the hook slot is aligned perfectly to the noise-making angle of the face.

BILL OF MATERIALS

1	1 × 4″ pine, 8″ long	base
1	1/2 × 3″ pine, 5″ long	sides
2	1/4 × 1/2 × 5″ plywood	blade guides
2	1 × 1″ pine, 41/2″ long	body guides
1	12″ hacksaw blade, 32 teeth per in.	
2	3/4 × 2″ dowel	handles
2	1/8 × 1″ stove bolts, w/nuts	
	3d finishing nails	
	white glue	
	epoxy cement	
	tagboard for shims	

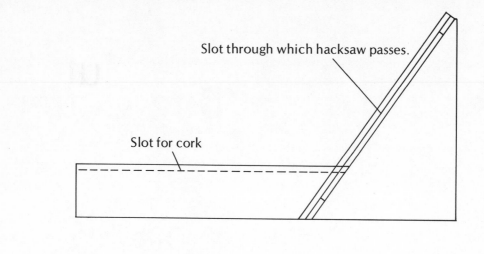

Slot through which hacksaw passes.

Slot for cork

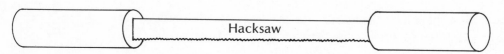

Hacksaw

Side view of bug cutter
showing base, blade
guides, and blade (not in
position).

First take the base piece and draw a center line down its length. Since the actual width of the nominal 4-inch board is 3½ inches, this will mean that the line will be 1¾ inches from either side. Once the line is drawn, tack the base to either the workbench, a saw horse, or a heavy piece of lumber. It must be immobile while you perform the next step.

Hold your rip saw parallel to the top of the base, and cut a groove ⅜ inch deep, that is, halfway through the base of the cutter. To get this line straight, you may find it helpful to tack a piece of scrap lumber along the side of the line to keep the blade of the saw from wandering and tearing up the surface of the board. Remove the guide strip and sand the surface of the base, running the paper down into the groove so that it has no jagged edges.

To make the sloping sides of the cutter, take the 5-inch piece of ½ × 3 and draw a diagonal line from one point to its opposite point. Cut along this line with the crosscut saw. The result will be two right triangles precisely the same size, with only one cut. This is the surest method of cutting two precise triangles. In order to get the slope side as smooth as possible, lay a sheet of 100 grit sandpaper on your workbench, or other hard surface, and rub the sloping side of the triangle (the cut side) flat against the paper. Repeat using 220 grit. Now install the sides against the sides of the base as shown in the illustration, using white glue and finishing nails.

Cut twelve ¹/₂-inch squares from the tagboard. These will be used as shims to hold the blade guide rails away from the slope of the sides to give the blade clearance. Glue these onto the slope of the sides at the four points shown in the diagram, three at each point, and allow the glue to dry thoroughly. Now take two ¹/₂-inch-wide strips of ¹/₄-inch plywood and, with glue and ¹/₂-inch brads, affix them to the sides, driving the brads into the sides through the shims. The brads will prevent the shims from working loose, and the glue will prevent the blade guides from wobbling.

Next make the cork guide. It would be nice if all of the corks used on popping bugs were the same size, but they aren't, and this means that you will have to make the guide for the cork size that you use most—or, if you wish, you can make bug cutters in different sizes for different-size corks. At a cost of about 50 cents for the entire cutter, it's pretty hard to go wrong. At any rate, the cork guide is essential for centering the hook slot. Take the two 4¹/₂-inch pieces of 1 × 1-inch pine. Now measure your cork at its widest point, and center that measurement on the groove in the base—for example, if your cork measured ³/₄ inch, then you would make a mark ³/₈ inch from each side of the slot. Make several of these marks along the length of the slot to assure that the guides will be perfectly parallel to one another. Now glue the two 4¹/₂-inch pieces with their inner sides along these marks, and nail them down with 3d finishing nails. You might think that by simply tacking them lightly you could move them around to take care of different-size corks; don't. They won't be stable enough, and after you have moved them back and forth a few times they won't hold at all.

Now take the hacksaw blade and break it into two sections, one of the sections 4¹/₂ inches long, the other 7¹/₂ inches long. This is quite simple to do; just make a mark on the blade at the point at which you wish it broken, grasp the blade on either side of the mark with two pairs of pliers, and bend. The blade is rather brittle and will break quite cleanly and easily. Coat the smooth edge of the shorter section of blade with epoxy cement, and install it in the slot in the base with the rounded end against the edge of the base farthest from the slope.

Now take two 2-inch sections of ³/₄-inch dowel, and, with the coping saw, make a slot down the center of each, halfway through the length of the dowel. These will be the handles of the longer section of the hacksaw blade. Fit the ends of the hacksaw blade into these slots, and drill two ¹/₈-inch holes, one in each handle, perpendicular to the slot and through both the wood and the hacksaw blade. Affix one of the handles to the blade with a ¹/₈ × 1-inch stove bolt and

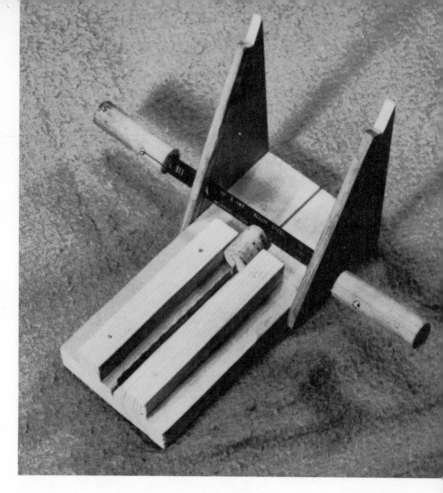

nut. Remove the other handle, slip the blade through the slots in the blade guide, and affix the other handle with another bolt. These handles prevent the blade from slipping out of the slot, and they make the cutting much easier on the hands as well. The fingers can get awfully tired pinching the end of a flat hacksaw blade through 15 or 20 corks at a sitting.

Those are the construction details. Here's how the bug cutter is used.

Take the cork, and place it on the hacksaw blade in the base between the guide rails. Grip the upper ends of the cork between your thumb and forefinger and rub the cork back and forth on the blade. As the blade bites into the cork it will sink lower and lower. The guide rails will keep it centered on the blade so that the cut is at a precise right angle to the cork face.

When the slot is deep enough, slide the cork forward, lift the section of the blade with the handles so that it just clears the cork, and move the cork so the blade just touches the top edge of the cork.

Enough of the cork will still be held on the slot cutter to keep it aligned. Now simply saw down through the cork. The entire procedure takes less than 30 seconds, and the result is a much more perfectly aligned popper body than you could hope to get by hand. Now finish the bug in the normal manner. If you turn out any more than one or two popping bugs at a sitting, this is a very worthwhile gadget to have around.

15

Live Bag

Although many people know that a fish out of water will die and spoil very quickly, not many know that an injured fish that dies in the water, especially in the summer, will spoil even more quickly than one left in dry air. Stringers do not keep the fish alive, and can actually injure them further. This is not so true of the chain/clip type, but the old style of stringer, a cord run through the tender gill filaments and out the mouth, will kill a fish quickly, and is best not used.

Commercial fishermen use live cars—large boxes that allow water circulation and give the fish room to swim around. Few fishermen could afford or handle such apparatus, and if you are just taking a few fish for personal use, they really aren't needed. You can make an excellent live bag yourself, completely, for about 75 cents, and you can make it to your own specifications. The live bag permits the fish a certain amount of swimming, and has the extra advantage of being able to be lowered into the cooler depths, instead of remaining in the sun-heated surface water as happens to stringers.

In order to make the live bag, you will have to learn one of the oldest crafts in existence—the weaving of a net. You can, if you wish, purchase a piece of netting, stitch it together in a cylinder, and proceed from there, but making your own netting is rewarding and relaxing. If you learn to tie the netting knot, you can carry a loaded shuttle in your tackle box and repair any holes that get in your landing net, before that lunker slips through them.

	BILL OF MATERIALS	
½ lb.	No. 12 bonded nylon	live bag
½ lb.	No. 7 or No. 9 bonded nylon	net bag
3	live bag rings	supports
1	large split ring	bottom closure
18″	No. 4½ nylon cord	

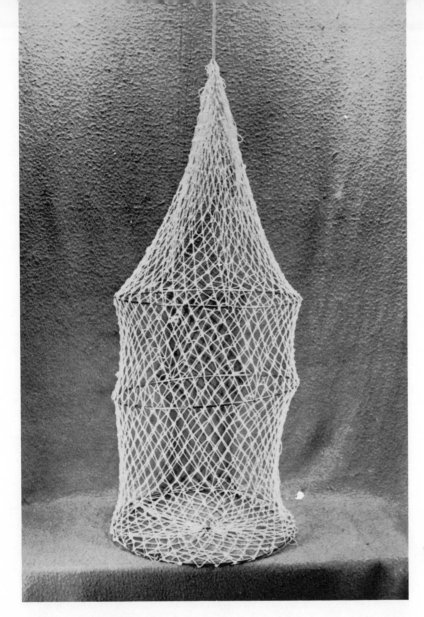

A live bag keeps the catch fresh.

You will need special tools for net weaving—a shuttle to hold the line and a gauge to determine the size of the meshes. You can make your own weaving tools. However, with the cost of a Delrin plastic shuttle at about a quarter and a good plastic gauge at around 15 cents, it is a waste of time to build them. These tools, along with bonded nylon twine (very good, because the nylon lasts a long time and the bonding helps prevent slippage of the knots) and various netting accessories, can be obtained from the Netcraft Company. The tools alone can be obtained from Herter's. Various commercial net manufacturers also supply all you would need, but often their minimum orders are far too high for the sportsman who simply wants to make a net bag or two.

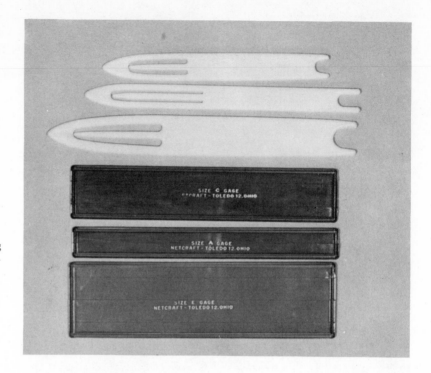

Three shuttles for weaving and three gauges for measuring mesh size.

For the live bag you will need a medium shuttle and a 1-inch gauge. This will make a net with a mesh size 1-inch square. You will also need approximately ½ pound of No. 12 bonded nylon. You can use heavier if you like, but it isn't necessary, since the No. 12 has a breaking strength of 112 pounds, and its smaller diameter means that you can get more on the shuttle, so that you will need to reload the shuttle less often.

To load the shuttle (see illustration) make a turn around the center post, bringing the line down so that it crosses the free end of the nylon. Bring the line down to the bottom of the shuttle, up the other side, around the flexible center post, and back down and under again. Continue in this manner until the shuttle is full. After a time you will get to the point where, simply pushing the center post back and forth with your thumb as the line comes up the proper side, you can wind the shuttle very quickly.

Now start the net. Screw a heavy cup hook into a wall, a window frame, or the workbench. You will be netting this in the flat, so you have to make a starting chain to determine the number of meshes. You can purchase a special tool from Netcraft, the Netcraft Wheel, which would eliminate this step, but the wheel costs approximately $5. If you have a sportsman's club, or intend to make quite a

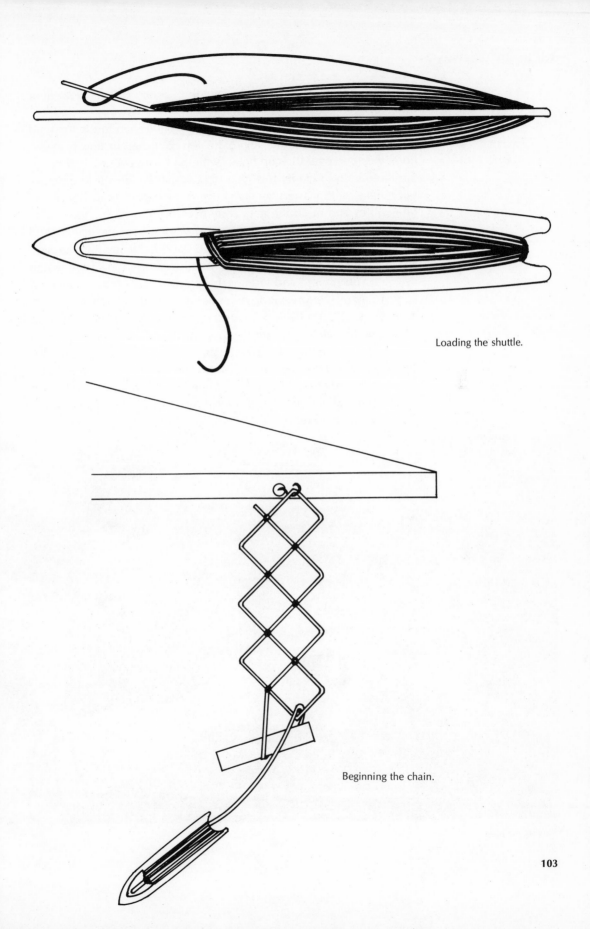

Loading the shuttle.

Beginning the chain.

few nets, it may be worthwhile investing in one of these excellent little devices.

To make the starting chain, tie a perfection loop in the free end of the line on the shuttle, approximately 2 inches in length. Now, hook this loop over the cup hook, with the knot to your left. Refer to the illustration to clarify this next step, which is difficult to describe but quite easy to master: lay the gauge at the bottom of the loop. The line will extend off to the left, away from the knot. Bring the shuttle down, across the gauge on your side, up under the gauge and through the perfection loop, and down over the gauge on your side again, pulling it tight. Now pinch the lines at the top of the gauge between your thumb and forefinger, and tie a sheet bend, or netting knot. To do this, throw a loop of loose line from the shuttle to the left, bring the shuttle up behind the *two* right-hand threads of the tine at the top of the gauge, through the loop that was cast to the side. Then pull the shuttle to the right and down, rolling the thumb and forefinger to make certain that the knot forms on the top of the mesh you just knitted, rather than beneath it. If the knot is on top, it is a proper sheet bend and will not slip. If it forms underneath, it is simply a slip knot, and no good for a net.

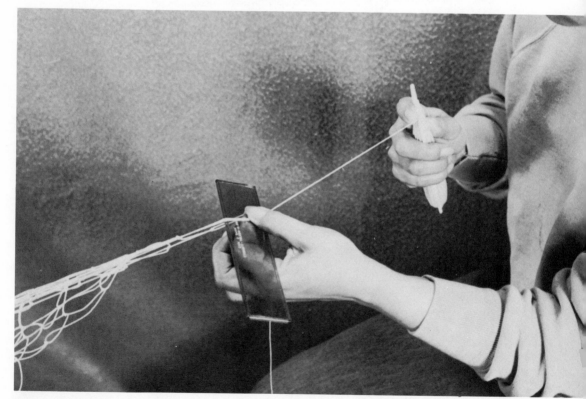

Gauging the mesh.

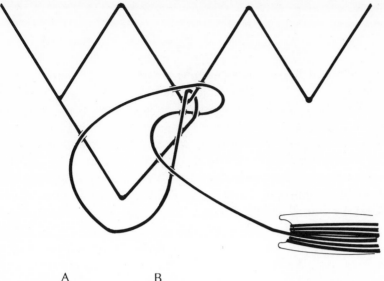

Top shows how to weave the netting knot. Inset "A" shows a properly formed netting knot, tied on top of the mesh. "B" shows a knot that has slipped below the mesh, forming a slip knot which will ride and cause the meshes to change sizes.

A   B

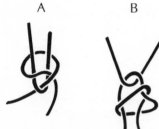

Roll the left thumb and forefinger to make sure the knot forms on top of the mesh.

I know that that sounds horribly complicated, but don't be discouraged. When I first started it took me close to two hours to get the first knot right. Now I knit an entire live bag in that time. Persevere!

Now take the perfection loop off the cup hook, and turn it over. Knit another mesh. Turn it over again, and knit another. Proceed in this manner until you have tied 76 knots. It seems like a lot, but you can do it in about 15 minutes once you master the knot, and once you pick up speed, in about 7 to 8 minutes. With the 76 knots, you have now knitted two rows of 38 meshes each. This is your basis for the bag.

Now the fun starts. Take a long metal rod, or a wooden dowel thick enough so it won't bend. Slide this through one of the rows of meshes, making certain that all of that row of meshes are on the rod. Now suspend the two ends of the rod, either behind two bent nails or in two screw eyes, so that the shuttle containing the line hangs straight down at the left-hand side. Using the gauge, and making the sheet bend netting knot as before, knit a whole row of 38 meshes. Turn the rod over so that the shuttle is again at the left, and make another row. If you are proceeding correctly with the gauge and the knot, all the neat little diamonds of the meshes should be the same size, and you should be able to tug gently at any point on the net without having any of the knots move.

Proceed in this manner until you have knitted a total of 48 rows of meshes. I know that, to someone who has never knitted a net before, 1,824 knots seems like an awful lot. Rest easy. Netcraft has a manual of nets that you can make, including a cast net as used in the South Sea Islands that contains *20,000* knots!

Now you will start decreasing the number of meshes. On the 49th row, at every 11th mesh, when you bring the shuttle up, go through both the 12th and the 11th mesh together, thus turning the two of them into a single mesh. Then knit a row without decreasing, and on the next row, knit every 10th and 11th mesh together, then another row without decreasing. Continue in this manner, dividing the remaining number of meshes evenly into four parts, until there are only 22 meshes left. Knit three rows with this number, and the hard part is done.

Now make a seam. Refer to the diagram for instructions. Do not use the gauge here—just estimate. You will have been looking at so many 1-inch meshes that you will be surprised at the accuracy you obtain when estimating the joining meshes. Take special care here to make certain that the knots don't slip.

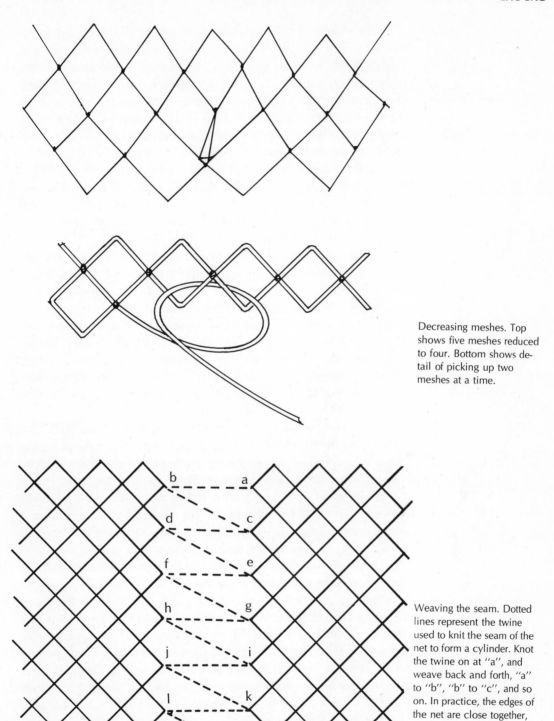

Decreasing meshes. Top shows five meshes reduced to four. Bottom shows detail of picking up two meshes at a time.

Weaving the seam. Dotted lines represent the twine used to knit the seam of the net to form a cylinder. Knot the twine on at "a", and weave back and forth, "a" to "b", "b" to "c", and so on. In practice, the edges of the net are close together, and the finished seam is indistinguishable from the rest of the net.

Now take a large split ring, and weave all 22 of the lower meshes to it with half hitches. Because of the small size of the ring you can't do this with the shuttle. Just take a 1-foot length of the twine, and carry out the weaving process with your fingers. Now take three live bag rings, obtainable from the Netcraft Company, 14 inches in diameter, and install them evenly spaced in the bag, again using half hitches to weave them to the meshes. You can use either the shuttle or your fingers here, whichever is easiest for you.

All that remains is to install a pucker string through the meshes at the top. Make this out of No. 4½ hard nylon cord. This will draw the top of the bag closed. Make it long enough so that you can tie the ends securely to an oarlock while allowing the full depth of the net to be beneath the surface of the water. Now take it fishing.

I said in Chapter 9, on the wooden trout net, that I would tell you how to make your own bag for the net. Here we go. Use No. 9 bonded nylon twine—the finer diameter is all that is required with a net of this size. And the bonded nylon net will handle better in the water. Make a starting chain of 34 meshes, using a 1¼-inch gauge and a medium shuttle. You will find that, with the fence staples spaced exactly 1¼ inches apart on the frame, you will have precisely 34 staples altogether, and by making a net with 34 top meshes there will be no need to double meshes when weaving them to the staples, as you would have to do with a purchased net.

This chain of 34 meshes, of course, involves tying 68 knots, since in making the chain there are 2 rows of meshes. Now place the chain on the rod or dowel and begin knitting. Now make 6 more rows of knots, all equal in length to the 34-mesh chain. From row 7 on, reduce one mesh in each row, as you did with the live bag, and make certain that the reductions do not come directly beneath each other. If they do, the finished net will not look as neat as it should, because the reducing weave naturally makes a bulky knot. As long as these are staggered, they are unnoticeable on the finished product. If they all come together, they make the bag look awkward.

Since you started with a 34-mesh chain, and will be reducing to 22 meshes in order to close the bottom to a split ring, this means that you will be knitting 18 rows of meshes altogether—6 standard after the starting chain, and 12 more with a single reduction in each. Now remove the net from the rod, close the seam as in the live bag, and whip the bottom closed to a split ring with half hitches. Then attach it to the net frame as per the instructions in Chapter 9.

Netting is a marvelous hobby, and a very relaxing way to spend the winter evenings when you can't actually go fishing. Many books have been written on the subject, and the Netcraft Company has a fine inexpensive manual of things to make once you have achieved the basic netting skills—a hammock, various sizes of landing nets ranging from minnow nets for bait to large boat nets for lake trout, tennis nets, that South Seas cast net if you have the time, even a shopping bag for the woman in your life.

16

Spinner Center

No, that isn't a square dance call. It simply occurred to me that, while there certainly are a goodly number of fly-fishermen and fly-tiers in existence, there are many, many more who fish spinners, and a fair portion of them make their own spinners and wire terminal tackle. Now, the description of building spinners and other tackle from wire, beads, brass and blades is so comprehensive as to warrant a book by itself. But this chapter is not dedicated to getting you interested in making your own. Rather, it is for the angler who already makes his own spinners, and doesn't have a set-up where he can store all his components near a good working space. This spinner center affords both a storage area and a work area which can be set on a table anywhere in the house. And since the actual bending and other metal work is done on the top of the storage area/work space, there is no danger of marring the table top.

The spinner center shown in the photographs utilizes an old silver chest for flatware which came from a junk shop. These are quite common, and can usually be purchased for around $2 or $3. I provide instructions for building the chest from scratch—with the exception of the ornate moldings it is the same as the chest in the picture—but since the lumber to make the case costs about as much as the discarded silver chest, I advise you to look for a silver chest first in junk or antique shops around your home, and save the time involved in building the case.

The main part of the case is built in approximately the same manner as the tackle box. Refer to Chapter 8 for primary construction details. However, when you get the box built, you will cut it differently.

BILL OF MATERIALS

2	¼ × 18½ × 10½" plywood	top and bottom
2	1" pine, 7" wide and 10½" long	ends
2	1" pine, 7" wide and 20" long	sides
1	¼ × 18½ × 10½" plywood	bin bottom
1	¼ × 17 × 9" plywood	drawer bottom
2	1" pine, 3" wide and 10½" long	drawer sides
2	1" pine, 3" wide and 17" long	drawer front and back
2	¼ × ¼ × 10½" plywood	support strips
6	wood screws	

(Drawer false front is made by cutting through box;
see text for instructions.)

1	2 × 3" whitewood or yellow pine 20" long	base for wire bender
5	16d or 20d common nails	studs for wire bender
3	medium brass hinges (or 1 18" piano hinge)	
3	small knobs, wood or porcelain	
	brads	
	white glue	
	stain	
	varnish or acrylic	
	felt	
	silicone rust preventative	
	4d finishing nails	
	compartmented plastic boxes, size, number, and style depending upon needs of user	

The spinner center.

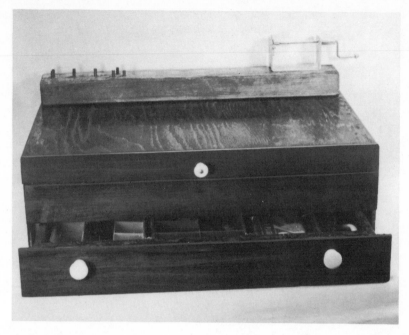

The basic box is cut in a different manner.

Build the main box. Make the sides of the box of regular 1-inch pine, and the top and bottom of ¼-inch plywood. Two more pieces of ¼-inch plywood form the bottom of the top compartment and the bottom of the drawer. Two pieces of 1 × 3″ measuring 2½ × 10½ inches and two pieces 3 × 17 inches form the sides, back, and front of the drawer. Do not nail one long side to the bottom.

After the box is built in the standard manner, cut through 1½ inches down from the top, to form the lid. Remove this and set it aside. Now, make one cut along one of the long sides of the box, 2½ inches from the bottom, and remove this piece. This is the drawer front, and should be easy to remove because it was the side that was not nailed through the bottom. Now construct the drawer with simple butt joints, using brads and glue, and slide it back into the case.

Now take two ¼-inch strips of ¼-inch plywood, and glue and brad them above the short sides of the drawer, making sure as you go along that they don't bind the drawer as it slides. If you varnish the inside of the case and the bottom of the drawer, you can then wax it

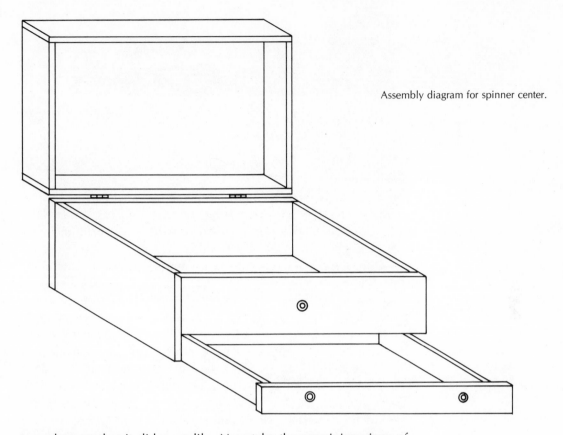

Assembly diagram for spinner center.

to make sure that it slides readily. Now take the remaining piece of plywood and glue it to the ¼-inch strips. This provides clearance so that the drawer will not bind on the bottom of the upper compartment. Install the top in the standard manner, with either three regular hinges or a length of piano hinge, and attach a small handle to the front edge of the top for lifting (opening), and two small knobs on the drawer front. The main part of the case is done.

Now we will convert this chest, whether purchased or homemade, into a complete center for making spinners, trolling triangles, spreaders, and most of the other hardware that spin-fishermen use.

First, we must make the bending jig for heavy wire, which also serves as the mounting plate for a light-duty wire former. Both Herter's and Netcraft, among others, supply these small sheet-metal wire formers for about $5, and the one from Netcraft comes with a book. This is the tool used to make most spinners, springs, and the other terminal tackle fashioned from light wire. It needs a firm mount, especially when making springs. The height of the chest lets it be mounted and left set up for immediate use.

Take a 20-inch length of 2 × 3-inch wood, preferably not pine as

The wire bending jig
should be made of hard-
wood.

this piece will also serve as a bending jig and will be subjected to a certain amount of stress. Hardwood would be best, although it is getting increasingly more expensive. You can use what they call white wood, which is the heartwood of various softwood trees, just as well, since its close grain approximates hardwood in strength, and it is much cheaper than genuine hardwood.

Using the coarsest sandpaper you can find, at least 36 grit, rough up the bottom of this piece, and rough a similar-sized area along the rear of the top of the chest. Coat with white glue and glue the 2 × 3 to the top of the chest, flush with the rear edge. Open the top, and run 6 wood screws up through the top of the chest and well into the 2 × 3, arranging them in three pairs, one pair close to each end and one pair in the center. The screws are necessary, because the stress of bending heavy wire in the jig could easily tear the glued joint loose. The screws also pull the 2 × 3 down firmly against the top of the chest, and if done before the glue has set will form a much greater surface contact, and a much better glue joint.

This is all the major construction. Now put a finish on the box. Again, because of the beauty of wood grain, I much prefer a stain and varnish finish. Rub the stain in well after the box is smoothly sanded and all corners slightly rounded, to bring out rather than cover up the attractiveness of the grain pattern. Then apply several coats of a good grade of varnish or acrylic.

The commercial wire former is mounted with the edge of its base flush with the right-hand end of the 2 × 3. This gives full freedom of hand movement in turning the crank, and provides a place to rest the left hand while steadying the spinner being formed while pushing up on the thumb pad of the wire former.

At the left end of the 2 × 3, we will now make the bending jig for heavy wire. Drill pilot holes, somewhat smaller in diameter than a 20d nail, in the pattern shown on the template illustration. The pilot holes will keep the nail from splitting the wood. Practice on a scrap piece of 2 × 3 until you find the drill that will give a hole large enough to prevent splitting, but still have enough friction to hold the nail firmly. Since different woods possess different compression val-

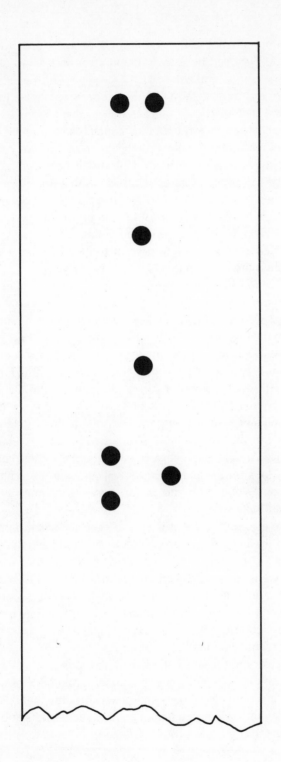

Template for wire bending jig. With the nails in these positions, you can carry out 90% of all heavy wire bending operations.

ues, I will not attempt to tell you the proper-sized holes to drill. You will have to discover those by trial and error on a scrap of the same lumber you used to make the jig.

When you have determined the proper-sized holes to use, drill them in the pattern shown, all the way to the bottom of the 2×3. Now drive the nails down until they contact the top of the chest, and cut off the heads of the nails so that ⅜ inch of the steel rod, with no head, protrudes above the block. These will be rough, so the next step will be to smooth them down. Begin with a fine cut mill bastard file, and then switch to successively finer grades of emery cloth until you reach crocus cloth and a very smooth finish with no roughness to snag or weaken the wire you will be forming. Coat these with a commercial silicone preparation to prevent rust—oil would seep into the wood around the nails and cause eventual softening.

The inside of the box can be set up in any way convenient for the type of work you do most, but I have a few suggestions that seem to work out well in general practice. Although wooden partitions can be put into the top, or even both, compartments, small beads and clevises can wedge down in the small cracks where they join the sides and bottom of the case. It is better, at least in my estimation, to outfit the case with plastic boxes of various sizes to contain the small gear used in spinner making. The seamless construction of the plastic boxes eliminates the wedging and loss of small paraphernalia, and the boxes can be taken out for closer scrutiny and selection of the proper parts. Another advantage is that, should the chest fall over, the individual tops on the plastic boxes will prevent the scattering and mingling of several thousand beads, clevises, spinners, propellers, blades, and bodies.

I have also found that it is best to keep the small parts, such as beads and the like, in the top compartment, and keep the tools such as wire crimpers and pliers, as well as the bulk wire itself, in the lower drawer. You don't need access to the tools and bulk wire as often as you do to the beads and so on, and it is easier to simply open the top than it is to slide yourself back, pull out the drawer, remove a plastic box, choose the proper piece, replace the plastic box, close the drawer, and slide back into position.

This case should satisfy the hardware fanciers who have looked with envy at the beautifully set-up cabinets and chests of the fly-tier, and at their scatterings of bags and boxes. It's time that spinner parts and equipment had a home just as good as the feathers and fur of the insect imitators.

17
Rod Rack

Hunters all have at least a rack to display their guns in, but how many of you fishermen out there keep your several hundred dollars' worth of rods and reels in a closet somewhere? The obvious answer is a wall display rack for your rods and reels. This one is quite simple and inexpensive to build.

```
┌─────────────────────────────────────────────────────────────────┐
│                        BILL OF MATERIALS                          │
│                                                                   │
│  1       1 × 8" pine, 48" long          sides and butt rack       │
│  1       1 × 4" pine, 17" long          upper rack                │
│  2       1 × 8" pine, 4" long           reel rack ends            │
│  1       1 × 17" dowel                  reel rack                 │
│  6       plastic rug protectors         butt holders              │
│  6       hose clamps                    reel holders              │
│  2       brass screw eyes                                         │
│          ¾" brads                                                 │
│          white glue                                               │
│          felt                                                     │
│          stain and varnish                                        │
│                                                                   │
└─────────────────────────────────────────────────────────────────┘
```

Lay out the pattern as shown on the 1 × 8, using the template provided as a guide for the curves. As you can see, the pattern has been designed so that the one 4-foot section suffices for both sides and the base without a bit of waste.

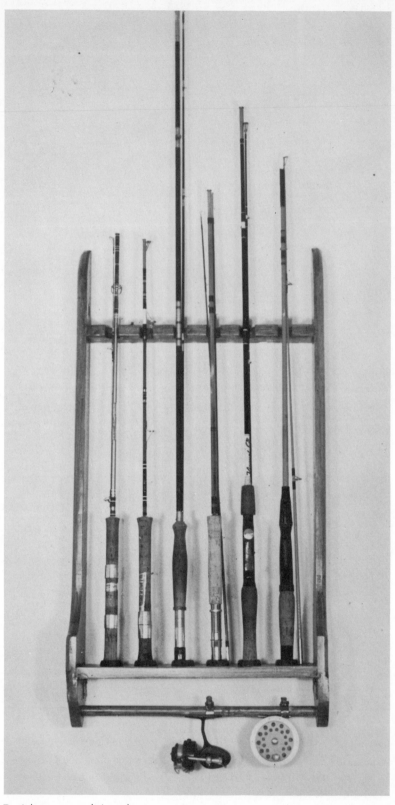

Don't keep your rods in a closet.

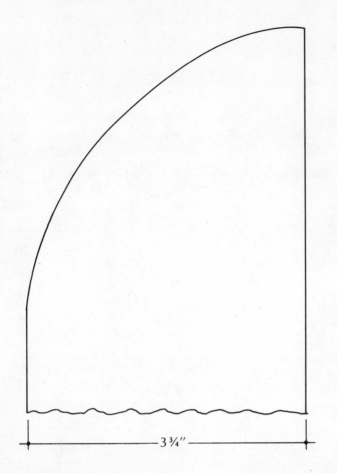

Template for curve on fishing rod rack. Bottom drawing shows how both halves of rod rack are laid out on one board. "c" is base of rack.

3 ¾"

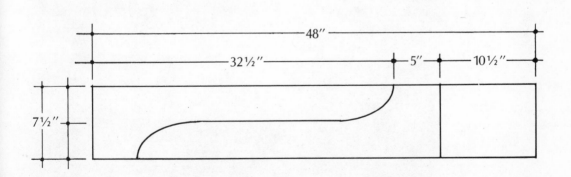

48"

32½" 5" 10½"

7½"

The completed rack, showing rug protectors in place and clamps on reel holder.

Now, on the 17-inch piece of 1 × 4, measure 1½ inches from one end, and cut a U-shaped notch with the coping saw 1 inch across and 1 inch deep. 1½ inches from that notch cut a second, and so on until there are six notches evenly spaced across the board.

Now assemble the rack in the following manner. Take the large ends of the sides, and nail the bottom to them, with the bottom on the *inside* of the sides. Measure up the sides 23 inches, and nail in the notched piece with the notches facing the front.

The rug protectors, as you may have guessed, are to hold the butts of the rods. Install them as follows. Put the rod in the rack, and line it up so it is perpendicular to the bottom. Now take a pencil and make a mark on either side of the butt of the rod.

Do this with each rod, placing it in the notch where you will want it to stay when the rack is finished. Now take the rug protectors and center them over the centers of those marks. Holding them in

Depth of Rack

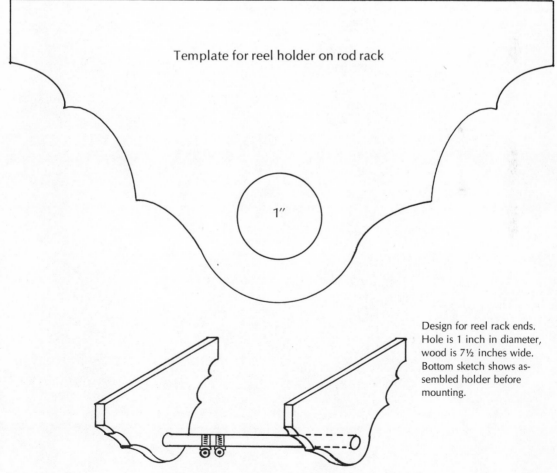

Template for reel holder on rod rack

1″

Design for reel rack ends. Hole is 1 inch in diameter, wood is 7½ inches wide. Bottom sketch shows assembled holder before mounting.

As assembled before attaching to rack.

121

place, drive two brads through each of them. The two brads will keep them from pivoting. Stain the rack, varnish it, and install one of the screw eyes 4 inches in from each end in order to give you something to hang it by.

I have included an extra diagram in case you want to display your reels along with the rods. To add this to the fishing rod rack, take 1 foot of 8-inch lumber and a 17-inch length of 1-inch dowel. Cut the sections as shown, glue and nail them to the bottom of the rack, and glue the dowel into the holes after slipping six 1½-inch hose clamps over it. Hook the reel into the hose clamp and tighten with a screwdriver so that the reel hangs below its respective rod. Stain and finish the reel rack like the rod rack, and you will have a display much like the fancy gun racks of the shooters.

III

FOR THE HUNTER

18

Custom Loading Bench

Reloading is to the shooter what fly-tying and tackle making are to the fisherman. The reloader-shooter can improve performance while saving money at the same time, or he can spend the same actual amount of cash and shoot a lot more than the nonloader.

There are certain problems to be faced in trying to save additional money through the building of your own equipment for reloading, however. The basic tools of handloading—presses, dies, scales, powder measures, and the like—are precision instruments which only the finest metalworker with the most sophisticated equipment could hope to manufacture effectively, and as such they are far beyond the realm of the average handy sportsman. However, several pieces of equipment do not require absolute precision, although they still, if purchased commercially, are expensive. I have dedicated this chapter to reloading equipment which will add to your enjoyment of the hobby at a very small cost, and in some instances even improve on the commercial versions of the same piece of gear.

I will not attempt to go into the basics of handloading your own ammunition. The subject is too complicated to cover in a book of this nature, and there are many excellent manuals on the subject. If you don't already reload, you might be interested in giving it a try. When you do, this chapter will be of use to you.

Perhaps the biggest problem faced by the beginning reloader is where to reload. If you use any of the small, hand-type reloaders, the kitchen table will suffice, although there is still the problem of where to store the components. When you progress to the full-size press-and-die combination, with powder scale, powder measure, case trimmer, and so on, you can't be hauling everything out of the closet

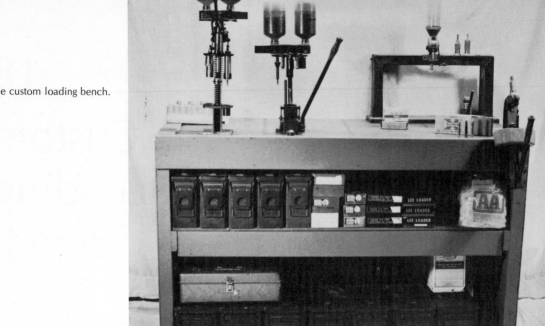

The custom loading bench.

every time you want to turn out ten or twenty new loads. You need a bench where everything can be set up and left that way.

A reloading bench is simple to build. There are no special joints, the materials are inexpensive, and, most important, the bench will be sturdy enough to permit the more vigorous operations of full-length resizing, case forming, and bullet swaging. The bench can be built in one day and the total cost might possibly run as high as $7.

	BILL OF MATERIALS	
4	2 × 4″ yellow pine, 36″ long	legs
4	2 × 4″ yellow pine, 43½″ long	side rails
4	1 × 4″ pine, 24″ long	end rails
1	¾ × 24 × 48″ plywood	top
1	¼ × 24 × 48″ plywood	shelf
1	1 × 6″ pine, 48″ long	face board
2	24 × 36″ Masonite	sides
1	36 × 48″ Masonite (optional)	back
8	12 × 12″ self-adhesive linoleum tiles	top covering
1 lb.	16d common nails	
1 lb.	1½″ ring-barb siding nails	

First, prepare the shelf and the top to be fitted to the 2 × 4s. This is accomplished by cutting a rectangle out of each corner of each plywood piece, the rectangle measuring $3^1/_2 \times 1^1/_2$ inches with the $3^1/_2$-inch measurement parallel to the 2-foot side of the plywood piece. You are now ready to assemble the bench, beginning with the legs. You will assemble the two ends of the bench in sections, and then use the shelves and the side rails to connect the two sections together.

Simplified drawing of bench construction. This is not drawn to scale, and it does not show a stage in the actual construction, but it gives some idea how the finished bench should look. For simplicity, the top, shelf, Masonite and face board have been eliminated from the picture. Attach the side rails as shown, but *not before the shelf and top are attached*. Inset shows method of notching shelf and top.

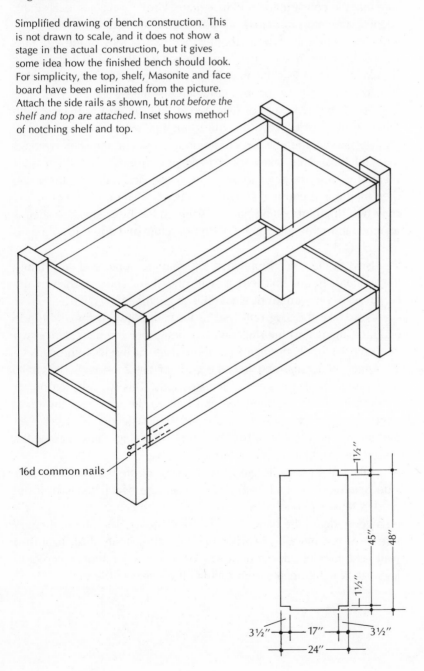

16d common nails

$3^1/_2''$ 17'' $3^1/_2''$

24''

$1^1/_2''$

45''

48''

$1^1/_2''$

Lay the 3-foot sections of 2 × 4 on the floor and measure ³/₄ inch from one end of each piece. This end will be the top of the bench. With a carpenter's square, draw a line across the 2 × 4 at this point. Do the same with each leg. *From that line* measure another 14 inches down each leg, and again scribe lines across the 2 × 4s. The second line marks the location of the shelf.

Set the legs in pairs, and join them, using the 1 × 4-inch end rails and ring-barb siding nails. Check frequently with the square to make sure that the construction will be square. Use four nails in each joint, keeping the nails as close as possible to the edges of the 1 × 4 without splitting the wood (about ³/₈ inch). The tops of the end rails should be aligned with the lines scribed on the legs; that is, one should cross the legs ³/₄ inch below the top of the legs, the other should cross them 14 inches below the first line.

Stand the two pairs of legs up, so that the end rails face each other on the inside. Now take the ¹/₄-inch plywood shelf and fit it to the legs, so that the notches fit around the legs and the shelf overlaps the end rails. This takes some jockeying around, and the easiest method is to fit the shelf to one pair of legs and nail it to the 1 × 4, then lift the free end and attach it to the other end of the bench. Use only two ring-barb siding nails in each end at first. After the shelf is attached to both ends, square up the structure and add six more nails to each end.

Now fit the ³/₄-inch plywood top onto the upper end rails, fitting the notches around the legs as with the shelf, and attach it to the bench with a minimum of eight nails in each end.

Now take the side rails and fit them in between the 1 × 4-inch end rails, up against the shelf and top, both front and back. Drive two 16d common nails through from the outside of the legs, through the 1 × 4-inch end rails, and into the ends of the 2 × 4-inch side rails, centering them in the ends of the side rails. This was the reason for keeping the nails fastening the end rails to the legs near the outer edges—to give free passage to the side rail fasteners. Nail the shelf and the top to the side rails using ring-barb siding nails, spacing the nails 2 inches apart.

Attach the Masonite pieces to the ends of the bench. These provide rigidity to the ends and help to keep the bench squared. If desired, a Masonite back can be installed on the bench, and this might be a good idea if the bench is to be freestanding. The one in the picture does not have a Masonite back because it sits flush against a wall, and therefore does not need a back, either for appearance or to keep small components from rolling off the rear of the shelf.

Attach the facing board to the front of the bench, nailing it to the 2 × 4 side rail so that ¼ inch extends above the top of the bench. This small lip will prevent spilled shot and primers from rolling forward off the bench, and spills can be slid forward to the lip where they can easily be picked up.

Finally, apply the self-adhesive tiles to the top of the bench, and give all exposed wood a coat of paint. The tiles provide a surface that is easily cleaned and will not stain or pick up powder granules and hold them, and the paint simply adds to the finished appearance of the bench.

If you have a lot of really heavy case forming or bullet swaging to do, you can either run bolts through the rear side rails into the wall, or you can attach angle brackets to the legs and screw the bench to the floor.

The bench fits easily into a small area, yet nevertheless has ample room to set up your metallic press, one or two shotshell presses, powder scale, powder measure, and case trimmer. The shelf, and the floor area beneath the bench, permit you to store all of your components beneath your work area. There they are convenient, and they add weight to the bench to prevent it from tipping when swaging bullets or performing other operations requiring a great amount of downward pressure.

With the bench complete, now it's time to build a couple of accessories that will make reloading a bit easier, and save you some money in the process.

NO-DANGER RELOADING BLOCK

Before I am attacked by the commercial manufacturers of reloading blocks, let me make it perfectly clear that the blocks on the market are not dangerous. Properly used, they are quite safe. But there is an inherent danger in most loading blocks that is the fault of normal human carelessness on the part of the reloader. That is precisely what this loading block is designed to avoid. I might also add that this sort of block was available on the market in 1967 for $4.50, and I am certain that the price has increased by now. You can build one for about 15 cents.

There is no problem in the construction of the block. Basically, it involves drilling and gluing, and the block can be made in less than 30 minutes. It can be made to any size, to properly fit any metallic cartridges you might be loading.

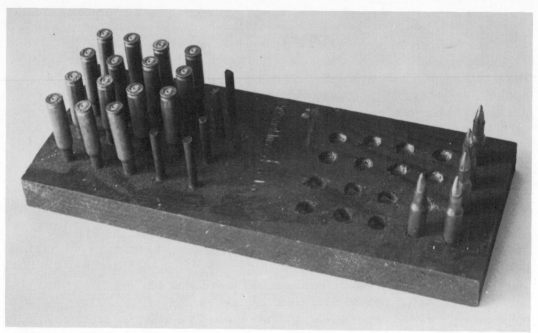

No-danger reloading block.

BILL OF MATERIALS		
1	1 × 6″ pine, 12″ long	base of block
20	2″ lengths hardwood dowels	cartridge holders
	white glue	

The diameter of the dowels for various cartridges can be found in the chart below. The size of the baseboard can be varied as well, although the size given above can be used for all except the largest calibers.

The chart does not take shotgun shells into consideration for one reason. Most presses perform a series of operations on the shell, taking it from fired to loaded condition without removing it from the press. If you use a style press which does not, then I refer you to Chapter 23 on building the shotshell trimmer, where dowel sizes for the various gauges are given, as well as sizes for the base holes.

Build the block in this manner. Measure the base of the cartridge, and multiply it by 4. Add 3½ inches. This is the width of the loading block. For example, if the base of the cartridge measures ½ inch, the width of the block would be ½ × 4 + 3½ inches, or 5½ inches—a standard 1 × 6 board. Now, multiply the width of the base of the cartridge by 5, add 4 inches, and double the result. This is the length of the block. Using the same example, the length would be

Dowel sizes and their corresponding calibers

Dowel size	Decimal equivalent	Calibers measuring
1/16	.0625	.17
1/8	.125	.17, .22
3/16	.1875	best for .22
1/4	.250	.257, .270, .284, .308 (7mm)
5/16	.3125	.303, .32, 8mm, .38 (.357)
3/8	.375	.375, .41, .44, .45
1/2	.500	large Blackpowder & Nitro Express cal.

($1/2 \times 5 + 4) \times 2$, or $6 1/2 \times 2$, or 13 inches. Therefore, the size lumber needed for the block would be $1 \times 6 \times 13$ inches. It sounds complicated, but it really isn't once you get the hang of it.

Cut a piece of lumber that size, and draw another rectangle inside it, 1 inch in from each edge. This is the border. Take a drill the size of the base of the cartridge, and measure 5/8 inch back along the

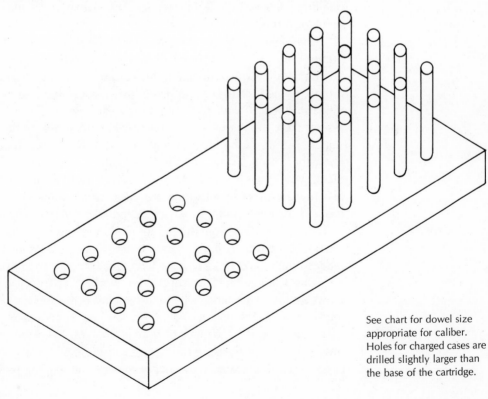

See chart for dowel size appropriate for caliber. Holes for charged cases are drilled slightly larger than the base of the cartridge.

bit from the point. At this point wrap several turns of masking tape around the bit to serve as a depth gauge, so that the drill will not go completely through the block. Drill four holes along one end of the block, using the inscribed rectangle as the outer edge guide for them, with ½ inch between each hole. Move ½ inch forward, and drill another line of four holes in the same manner. Proceed in this way until you have five lines of holes, or 20 holes in all.

Now refer to the chart a little way back and choose the size dowel which most nearly corresponds to the caliber of your cartridge. Take a dowel of this size, and cut twenty 2-inch lengths. With a drill bit of that size, make your depth gauge again, and drill 20 holes, evenly spaced, in five rows of four each, in the other end of the block. The spacing here will depend upon the size of the hole, but each of the holes should have the same center as the larger holes at the other end. An easy way to accomplish this is to line up the centers of one column of holes, and draw a line down the other half of the block. Do this for all the columns. Then measure the distance between the inscribed lines, and draw cross lines perpendicular to them across the width of the block. The intersections of these lines are the centers of the holes for the dowels.

Now take the 20 pieces of dowel, dip one end in white glue, tap one firmly into each hole, and let dry. The loading block may now be painted, varnished, or left as is.

The block is used in this manner. As the fired cartridges are deprimed and resized, they are placed neck-down over the dowels. Then, after they are all done and thus arranged, they are taken one at a time, primed, charged, and placed neck up in the base holes provided for them. If your press primes the cartridge at the same time it resizes the case, then they are merely charged at this point. The important feature of the block is that, if a cartridge is on the pegs, you know there is no powder in it; if it is mouth up at the other end of the block, you know it is already charged and ready for the bullet. The two human errors in reloading are cases which have been double-charged (deadly), and cases with no powder, which can drive the bullet into the barrel from the primer explosion and tie up the gun for the rest of the trip. With this sort of block, there is no doubt in the reloader's mind, and he can shoot with greater confidence as a result.

This loading block is superb for working up precision loads. However, there are times when the reloader is making up a series of loads in which the powder volume is so close to the capacity of the case that there is no danger of double charges. With the following small project, the measure stand/die rack, the loader can charge the cases much more rapidly by simply moving the loading block back and forth under the powder measure charging each case as it passes under the drop tube. In addition, for those without turret presses, it provides an excellent means of having the next die needed right at hand.

MEASURE STAND/DIE RACK

This is a combination project. It is not something that you couldn't buy, although the combination does not exist as such on the market. But you could purchase a powder measure stand for about $6, and a die rack for about $4; or, you could build this project in half an hour for about a quarter.

All you need is 4 feet of 2 × 4 and a piece of ¾-inch plywood, measuring 6 inches by 26 inches. Refer to the diagram for construction, because it can be seen much more readily than it can be described.

Measure stand/die rack.

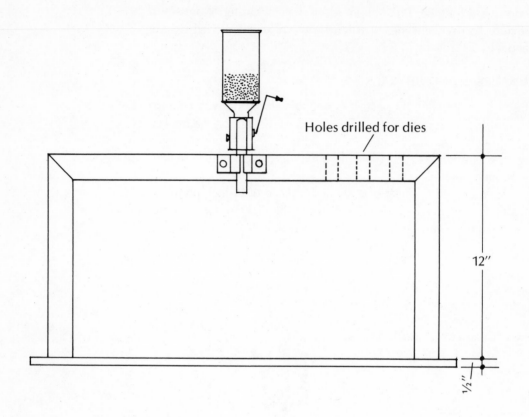

Holes drilled for dies

12"

½"

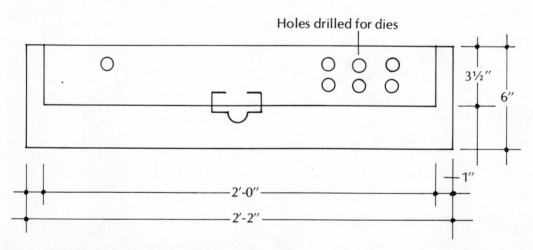

Holes drilled for dies

3½"

6"

1"

2'-0"

2'-2"

Frontal and overhead view of measure stand/die rack.

After the stand is put together, mount your powder measure in the center. This lets you run a loading block full length under the spout, charging one cartridge after another.

Standard reloading dies have a $\frac{7}{8} \times 14$ thread, so, along the top of the measure stand, drill a series of $\frac{7}{8}$-inch holes, keeping a $\frac{1}{2}$-inch space between them. The 2-foot length of the top bar of the stand will accommodate 24 holes (as shown in the diagram), enabling you to store, ready for use, either eight 3-die sets or twelve 2-die sets, or any combination thereof. The weight of the dies and the protruding lip of the base keep the stand stable, or it can be screwed to the bench if desired. Try it. It really makes reloading a lot more convenient.

The section of 2×4 makes the sides and top of the measure stand/die rack. These are fitted together with glue and screws. The bases of the two side pieces are flat. The top ends, as well as the ends of the die rack section, have mitered surfaces; that is, the joints are cut at a 45-degree angle, either with a power saw with a tilting base or with a handsaw in a miter box. The mitered corners serve two purposes: they give the stand an attractive finish, and they provide greater strength.

The piece of plywood is for the base. It is attached to the two uprights of the stand with four 3-inch wood screws, with the short sides of the uprights flush against one of the long sides of the base. The base provides an excellent place to leave the scale set up, since it will always be ready for checking thrown charges. The lip of the base which extends toward you in use provides greater stability for the stand when the charges are thrown, and in so doing automatically gives more consistent thrown charges.

You may paint this stand if you like. It is portable, but if it is painted the same color, or stained or varnished in the same manner as the reloading bench, when it is set up it will look like a built-in part of the reloading bench. But however you finish it, or even if you leave it unfinished, it is a handy accessory to have around whether you are running off a hundred plinking rounds for the '06 or a few long-range accuracy loads for the .222.

19

Custom-Fitted Shotgun Case

A few of the better gun makers in America offer shotgun cases as optional accessories with their better guns, although not with the cheaper models. They are both expensive and extremely heavy, but they afford the greatest protection available to the gun since it left the factory. However, fitted cases are only available for the most expensive guns to begin with.

Protect your shotgun with a custom-fitted case.

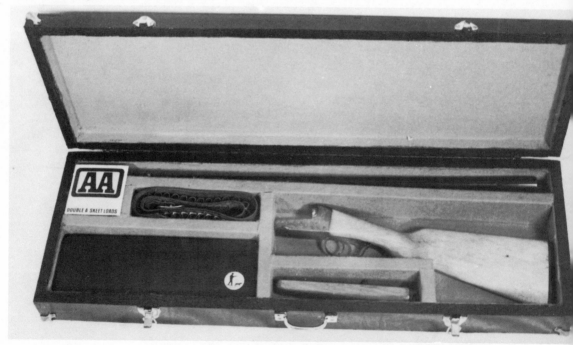

For a long time I have felt that this discrimination was unfair, not so much to the sportsman as to the less expensive guns which serve them so well. My favorite gun is a little Stevens 311 20-gauge double, a shotgun that has accounted for more game than any other gun in my collection. The Stevens has been with me since I was in my 'teens, and is as battle-scarred and beaten-about as I am, but it has given me more fond memories than anything else I have ever owned.

A gun like that deserves something more than a plastic sleeve to take its chances in, and I decided that I was the one to do something about it. So, working from the general style of the English fitted trunk case, I set about making a custom case for my long-time hunting companion.

This project is designed to be altered for your own gun. I will describe the procedures, and, since the Stevens double is quite a popular shotgun, I will give the dimensions for a case designed to fit that particular model. Using the general instructions and the measurements of your own gun, you will be able to adapt the case for any model or barrel length. The barrel length is what ultimately determines the overall length of the case.

BILL OF MATERIALS

2	¼ × 35½ × 12″ plywood	top & bottom
2	1 × 4″ pine, 10½″ long	ends
2	1 × 4″ pine, 35½″ long	sides
2 yds.	red (or other) felt	lining
1	1 × 3″ pine, 8″ long	dividers
2	medium brass latches	
1	medium brass handle	
1	30″ brass piano hinge	
8	round brass feet	
½ lb.	4d finishing nails	
	white glue	

Obviously, this is not one of the cheapest projects in the book, nor one of the simplest. But it says something for the other projects in that the case will take about 5 hours to build, and at a cost of between $5 and $6.

First, assemble the box as was done with the wooden tackle box in Chapter 8—that is, build it as an enclosed cube. Use simple butt joints, with the 1 × 4 × 10½-inch pieces in between the 1 × 4 × 35½-inch pieces, and use both glue and nails on the joints. (*Note:* If you elect to finish the box with wood stain instead of covering it with

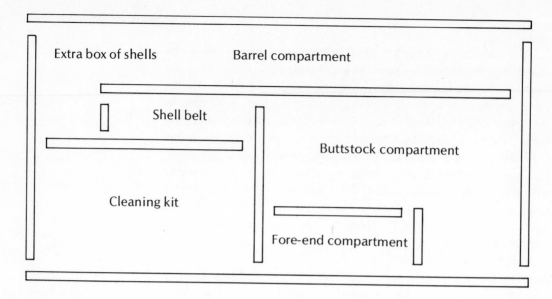

Extra box of shells

Barrel compartment

Shell belt

Buttstock compartment

Cleaning kit

Fore-end compartment

This exploded view drawing of the shotgun case is not to scale. All connections are simple, nailed butt joints.

vinyl like mine, I advise fitting the top and bottom inside rather than simply overlapping the sides. The two pieces of plywood thus must be cut smaller, to 34 × 10½ inches. Also, when measuring down from the top to scribe the line for cutting, measure only 1 inch instead of 1¼ inches as described below. This will compensate for the ¼ inch of inside space you lose by fitting the bottom inside, and the dividers will still align properly.) Now, in the same manner in which you separated the top from the bottom of the tackle box, measure down 1¼ inch from the top, scribe your line all the way around the box, and cut carefully through with the saw. Align the top and bottom of the case, clamp them together, and install the strap or piano hinge centered on the long side of the case.

There are three methods of finishing the outside of the case, each with its advantages and disadvantages. Read about all three before proceeding.

The first method covers the case with vinyl wallpaper. Place the box down flat. Cover the top of the box and the sides, *down to the cut,* with white glue. Place a piece of vinyl wallpaper over the glued area so that it extends down *past* the glue on all sides. Using a ruler, squeegee the wallpaper from the center to the edges, so that it makes full and flat contact with the glue, and so that there are no air bubbles to snag on something later and tear. If this is done properly, the box will be extremely durable. Trim the loose edges with a single-edged razor blade, cutting in toward the cut in the box so as not to lift the newly glued paper away from the edges. Trim around the hinge as well. Then turn the box over and repeat the gluing and trimming operation on the bottom of the case.

The advantages of this method are that the case will be water-repellent, the finish will be exceptionally strong, and the box will, with wood-grained paper, have the appearance of solid wood. The disadvantages are that the paper *is* difficult to apply with perfect smoothness, and even if the paper is perfectly smooth on the top and sides of the case the edges of the paper, which are raw where the case opens, have a tendency to get a bit ragged after a while.

The second method employs stain and varnish. A good grade of spar varnish will waterproof the case, but the construction methods make it impossible to get the proper appearance with stain. Plywood stains darker than lumber, and unless you have modified the assembly of top and bottom as described above, the exposed ends of the plywood give the finished box a Necco Wafer appearance. Nonetheless, stain and varnish are much easier to apply than the paper. You will still have to fill all the gaps in the edges of the plywood to prevent moisture from seeping down into the wood.

The third alternative is perhaps the best compromise between appearance and durability: painting. Certain preparatory measures must be carried out, however, before the case is painted. All gaps in the edges of the plywood must be filled to prevent the seepage of moisture between the plies. The case must then be sanded smooth. Fine sanding is not necessary in the case of the vinyl paper, but roughness on a painted case is certainly out of the question. Follow the procedures for all stained and varnished projects, beginning with coarse paper (50 to 80 grit) and working down the line to 220 grit garnet paper, finishing off with steel wool. Once the case is smooth, you can proceed with the painting.

Vinyl paper or stain with good marine varnish will flex somewhat, should the airlines accidentally drop or set something heavy on top of the case. Regular enamel will not. Standard enamel paints will ultimately chip, show hairline cracks, and footprints. A few products on the market can take care of the problem.

The first, and best, is epoxy paint. Epoxy will withstand everything except being run over with a fork lift, and makes an excellent, very attractive job. It is expensive, however.

If you don't wish to invest the money in the epoxy, several new vinyl paints have a gloss like fine enamel, and will serve. Not so durable as the epoxy resin paints, they nevertheless will take quite a beating before giving way.

Now a word on color, should you decide to paint. Since the case is yours, you may certainly paint it any color you choose. Much can be said for fluorescent orange when attempting to reclaim all your luggage at your destination. However, I recommend a black case.

The final appearance of the case—bright brass fixtures against a glossy black background—is something that anyone would be proud of. A red felt interior adds that much more richness to the black exterior.

Now it is time to install the rest of the hardware. This in itself is not difficult. One of the rounded brass feet should go on each corner. The rounded feet will help to keep the case up and away from sharp gravel and other snags the case is likely to encounter in the field. Install one of the latches 8 inches in from each end, and center the handle between them on the wide section of the case edge.

Now you are ready to customize the interior. The first step is to line it. Open the case, and coat the inside with white glue. In the same manner that the outside was covered with vinyl, cut oversized pieces of felt (corduroy, fake fur, or even velvet if your tastes run in that line), lay them over the glued area, and squeegee them outward so that they, too, make full contact with the glue. Take the razor blade again, cutting outward this time, and trim the material off flush with the edges of the case. (Tip: If you wait until the glue has partially dried the material will stiffen, and will be easier to cut without tearing.)

We're almost finished. Now, on the floor, lay out an area the size of the interior of your case (in the Stevens case, that area is 10½ × 34″ inches), and in that area place all of the accessories, including the gun, broken down, that you wish to carry. Leave 1 inch

The finished case. Compartment is lined completely.

between each accessory and its neighbor. Now take the 8-foot piece of lumber, and cut partitions together as a unit, and cover them with the same material with which you covered the rest of the inside of the case, but don't cover the bottom, or the ends of the partitions which butt against the walls of the case. Instead, coat these with glue, and install the partition unit inside the case. Now put in the accessories and you're ready to go.

The close partitions keep the accessories from rattling around; the inner material keeps the gun from being scarred or abraded; the outside finish effectively keeps water off; the brass feet prevent scarring of the case; and the heavy construction protects the gun and accessories when the airline uses your gun case for a trampoline.

As I've said, you can use any color for both the inside and outside, although the dark colors set off the brass hardware to much better advantage. Black with gold wide-wale corduroy interior is particularly rich-looking. My own holds the gun itself, a box of shells, cleaning kit, and shell belt. It makes trips a lot more pleasant when everything is right together, and when all you have to do is pick up one case and go, knowing that everything you need is right at your fingertips.

20

Game Carrier

Most hunters are well aware of the proper methods for handling game in the field—remove the viscera and, if the game is small, fill the body cavity with dry grass; or, if the game is large, prop the body cavity open with a stick to promote cooling. Many sportsmen have avoided the problems found with rubber-lined game pockets, which retain heat, by carrying along a length of cord with a ring at each end. After the game is field-dressed, they make sliding loops in the cord and hang the game from their belts, where the circulation of air will cool the meat quickly.

The game carrier, closed and open.

But what happens when the day is over and it's time for that long drive home? Nine times out of ten the game is simply chucked into

the trunk or the back seat, wrapped in a plastic bag. The heat is turned on in the car, the drive starts, and the meat approaches spoilage with every added mile.

It is not difficult to make a carrier for game that will keep it cool and preserve its freshness on the drive home.

BILL OF MATERIALS

1	¼ × 24 × 36" plywood	base
4	1 × 2" pine, 10½" long	vertical supports
2	1 × 2" pine, 24" long	top framing, ends
4	1 × 2" pine, 33" long	side framing, top & bottom
1	1 × 2" pine, 22½" long	bottom framing, rear
2	1 × 2" pine, 22½" long	door framing, top & bottom
2	1 × 2" pine, 9" long	door framing, sides
1	¼"-mesh hardware cloth, 10¼ × 22"	door screening
1	¼"-mesh hardware cloth, 11 × 23½"	end screening
1	¼"-mesh hardware cloth, 24 × 36"	top screening
2	¼"-mesh hardware cloth, 11 × 35"	side screening
2	brass hinges	
1	sliding bolt	
2	⅜" nylon rope, 8' long	
1	staple gun	
1	blanket or rug scrap, 24 × 36"	
8	brass L-brackets	
	6d finishing nails	
	brads	
	¼" staples	

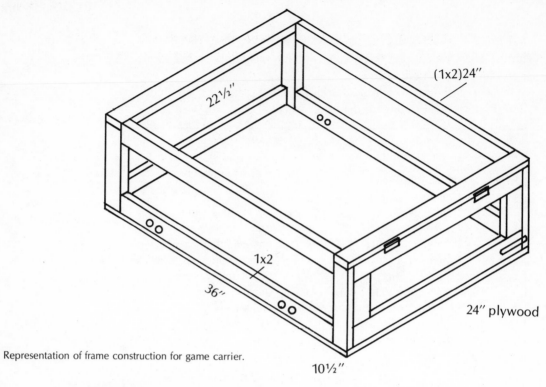

22½"

(1x2)24"

1x2

36"

24" plywood

10½"

Representation of frame construction for game carrier.

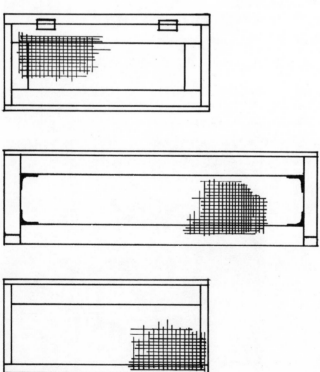

The staple gun required in construction may be too expensive to purchase for this project alone. However, tool rental businesses can supply these guns on a daily basis, at approximately $1 rental fee, and many hardware stores also rent staple guns to purchasers of hardware cloth and other screening at nominal prices.

The frame for the game carrier is constructed as shown in the diagram. Build the two end frames first, attaching the top end framing to the tops of the vertical supports. Turn these upside down, lay the plywood base on top of them so that they are flush with the ends of the base, and drive two 6d finishing nails through the base into each of the four vertical supports.

Turn the frame back over, and attach the side framing with the brass L-brackets, screwing the brackets to both the side framing members and the vertical supports. Nail the bottom framing, rear, in between two of the vertical supports at one end of the game carrier, driving the nails through the sides of the vertical supports into the ends of the framing.

The door is made in a simple frame with the sides placed between the top and bottom. On one side of the door frame thus constructed, staple the 10¼ × 22-inch door screening, making certain that there is a border of bare wood around each edge to prevent the screen from catching on the carrier frame when the door is opened and closed.

Attach the door to the end of the carrier without the bottom framing, with the two hinges at the top of the door. The screen side of

Hole positions for rope.

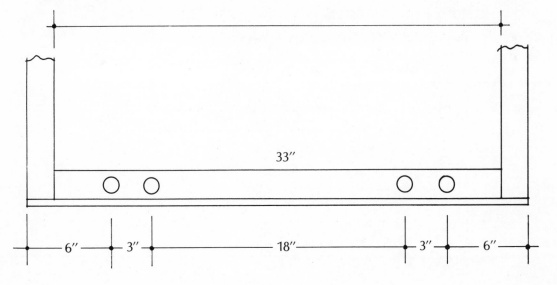

the door should be on the inside of the carrier. At the bottom of the door, to one side, attach the sliding bolt that serves to lock the carrier closed when in use. (There is no framing at the bottom of the door end of the carrier so that, in the event of rain, the door can be opened and the carrier tilted to allow the accumulated water to run out.)

Now attach the rest of the screening to the outside of the carrier. The slightly undersized pieces of screening prevent ragged edges from extending past the edges of the wood to catch in skin or clothing. Be liberal with the staples; they cost less than 80 cents per thousand, and the more you use the tighter the wire will hold.

Now bore four ½-inch holes in each side of the lower carrier side frame, as shown on the diagram; turn the carrier over and drive brads through the plywood into the bottom members of the framing. Be careful not to drive any through the end containing the door. The reason for installing the screening before nailing the bottom is that the screen gives extra support to the frame for the nailing operation.

To use the carrier, center it on the roof of your car over the section of blanket or carpet (to protect the car's paint) and run one end of one of the nylon cords through one of the pairs of holes in the framing as shown on the inset drawing. Run the other end of the cord through the car windows, and repeat the operation on the corresponding pair of holes on the other side of the carrier. Even up the cord, and tie the ends together, snugging the carrier down against the car. Repeat the entire operation for the other sets of holes, and the carrier is ready to bring home the makings of pheasant under glass—with no chance of spoilage.

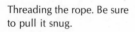

Threading the rope. Be sure to pull it snug.

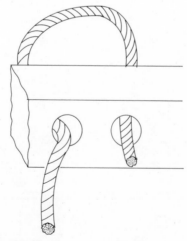

21
Shotshell Carrier

Carrying ammunition from one point to another can be a problem. For the shotgunner, it is a big problem because his ammunition is much larger and because he needs to carry more shells. The boxes in which shotgun shells are packed are certainly pretty to look at on the store shelves, or on the shelf of your gun closet; they are about as durable as egg shells, however. And although modern shotshells are waterproof, the boxes most assuredly are not, and have a disconcerting habit of disintegrating in a wet duck blind and strewing the shells all over the floor.

Shotshell carrier keeps shot dry.

It is relatively easy, however, to build a shotshell case that will transport 100 shells at once, that will not fall apart should rainwater hit it, that will serve to transport the spent shells home for reloading (have you ever tried to get 25 spent shells back into one of those factory boxes?), and which allows you to remove the shells one by one, with the heads all facing in the same direction, for transfer to a shell vest, hunting coat, or reloading tray.

If you are a dedicated scatter-gunner you have probably already built the custom-fitted shotgun case. You may even have built the wooden tackle box from the fisherman's section. Those projects should have given you enough practice in the style of building boxes so that you can proceed with this project without any problems. If you have not built any of those other projects as yet, refer back to Chapter 8 for the procedure involved in building the box and cutting it in half.

BILL OF MATERIALS

2	⅛" Masonite, 5½ × 10½"	shell racks
2	⅛" Masonite, 7 × 12"	top and bottom
2	1" pine, 7" wide and 12" long	sides
2	1" pine, 7" wide and 5½" long	ends
4	⅜" plywood, ½ × 5"	rack supports
2	brass latches	
2	2" brass hinges	
1	medium handle	
	3d finishing nails	
	brads	
	white glue	
	enamel	

These measurements are given for the middleweight in the shotgunning field, the 20-gauge. If you shoot a 12-gauge, increase the length and width by 2 inches. The depth can remain the same, since both shells are 2¾ inches long. Should you be partial to the sore shoulders that come from belting away with the 3-inch magnum shells, increase the depth measurement of the case by 1¼ inches. On the other hand, should you be involved in the growing sport of mini-skeet, and need a case for the 3-inch .410 shells, then decrease the length and width by 1 inch, and increase the depth by 1¼ inches.

Because the four sizes of shells mentioned above are the most often used today (the once popular 16-gauge is dying, and the handy little 28-gauge is a gun for experts), those are the only particular dimensions I will mention. A case for either can be built, certainly, and there is no need to build a case of different overall dimensions;

simply use the 12-gauge case for the 16's, and the 20-gauge case for the 28's, altering the size of the holes in the racks to fit the particular casing.

To simplify matters, the finished sizes of the three major carriers will be as follows:

12-gauge:	$14 \times 8 \times 7\frac{1}{4}''$
20-gauge:	$12 \times 7 \times 7\frac{1}{4}''$
.410 bore:	$11 \times 6 \times 7\frac{1}{4}''$

Build the box in accordance with the instructions given for the wooden tackle box, using butt joints so that the ends go inside the sides. However, the Masonite pieces overlay the sides and ends instead of being inserted between them as in the case of the top and bottom of the tackle box. Use glue and 3d finishing nails, and then cut through the box in the same manner described for the other box projects, 1 inch down from the top, and install the hardware. If there is any question as to how this is to be done, refer again to Chapter 8, which includes the details on mounting the latches and hinges and centering the handle.

Now you are ready to make the actual shell carriers. Take the two pieces of Masonite designated as racks, and drill 50 holes in each, allowing ½-inch margins around the outer rim of the racks and ¼ inch between each hole. The sizes of the holes should be as follows:

12-gauge:	$^{13}/_{16}''$
20-gauge:	$^{11}/_{16}''$
.410 bore:	$^{15}/_{32}''$

A power drill with a bit of the proper diameter makes the work go a lot faster, but it can easily be done with a brace and bit. To make things a lot easier, take a scrap of lumber the same size as the Masonite racks and place it on the workbench. Now take the two pieces of Masonite, line them up perfectly, and lay them on top of the scrap. Drive a 3d finishing nail through each corner so that the pieces are pinned to the scrap, and leave about a half inch of the nails protruding. Now you only have to drill 50 holes instead of 100, since the bit will go through both pieces of Masonite perfectly, with the scrap wood preventing it from going into the workbench. Pull the nails out, and you have two separate and perfectly drilled shell racks.

Now take two of the rack supports and tack them in with brads so that the upper edge of the plywood pieces is 2½ inches above the bottom of the case. Coat the upper edges of these pieces with glue, and position one of the Masonite shell holders on top of the two rack supports. This will be the permanent shell holder.

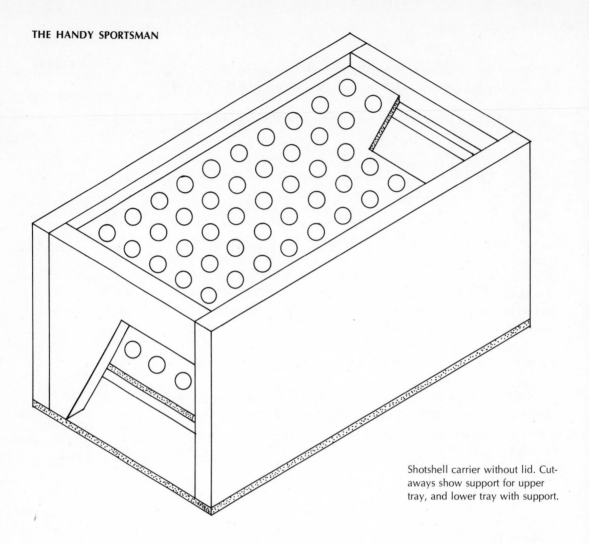

Shotshell carrier without lid. Cut-
aways show support for upper
tray, and lower tray with support.

Now take the other two strips and position them so that their
upper edge is ⅛ inch below the upper edge of the bottom section of
the case itself. The other shell rack simply rests on top of these, and
since it is positioned ⅛ inch below the edge of the case, it fits flush
with that edge, so that the bottom half of the case when opened is
smooth from side to side with no flange of case sides or ends extending above the removable rack. This gives the case a neat appearance, and the upper shell rack can be removed when necessary to
gain access to the 50 shells in the permanent holder below.

Now coat the shell racks, as well as the interior and exterior of
the case, with a good grade of enamel. Apply at least three coats so
the build-up will shed water should the case inadvertently be exposed to rain. You can use epoxy enamel, but since this case is not
usually carried into the field with you, but rather left in the car for

storage of extra shells, I doubt whether the increased durability of the epoxy enamel is worth the increase in cost over regular exterior oil-base enamel.

Finally, remove the upper shell holder, and fill the bottom with 50 shells. The holes are designed so that the shells will catch on the rim. Then set the removable holder back in the case, and fill it with another two boxes of shells. You now have a very durable yet portable case that holds four boxes of shotgun shells—and the empties can be replaced in the holes and carried home. A case similar to this one, slightly lighter because it is made from plastic, costs about $8 in sporting goods stores; yours will run about $1. And if you don't think you need a case like this, just pay attention to the way your paper boxes behave the next time you have to carry several on a long trip or into a duck blind.

The case also serves two other functions. It can readily be set up on a bench for patterning different loads through your gun (which should be done to determine which loading gives the greatest evenness of pattern at various shooting ranges). And it really comes in handy when it's time to reload those hulls. Just take the spent case out of the box, reload it, and drop it back in the same hole. When the last shotshell is reloaded, so is the carrying case, and you're all ready to go again.

22

Trapshooter's Box

Naturally, the trapshooter can use the shotshell carrier described in the previous chapter, but there are times when such a device may be inconvenient, for the simple reason that the shotshell carrier takes time to load and unload, and also a certain amount of moving around—time and freedom which the hunter may have, but which the trapshooter in competition well may not have. With the trap-shooter's box, spent shells may simply be tossed into the center; it is

Trapshooter's box is handsome and functional.

also easier to grab up when moving from station to station. Made with the 12-gauge in mind, since that is the gauge most frequently used for trapshooting, it is more than ample for 16- or 20-gauge shells. You can, if you desire a specially-fitted trapshooter's box, cut the size down to fit the smaller shells, but I will leave that decision up to you. In making the box smaller, you cut down on the size of the area which holds the spent casings. With the cost of good hulls and the rules of many trap clubs to the effect that any case hitting the ground automatically belongs to them, you can't afford to miss the mark with the empties any more than you can afford to miss the bird with the shot string.

There are no real difficulties in construction, and the box can be made for about 75 cents worth of lumber. The builder can substitute plywood for the 1-inch pine if he desires, but the finished appearance of the box is much better when regular lumber is employed.

	BILL OF MATERIALS	
2	$1 \times 6''$ pine, 15" long	sides
2	$1 \times 6''$ pine, 7¼" long	ends
1	$1 \times 10''$ pine, 13½" long	handle/divider
1	$1 \times 8''$ pine, 13½" long	bottom
	4d finishing nails	
	plastic wood	
	white glue	
	stain	

Assemble the box with the sides overlapping the ends so that the actual outside dimensions of the box are $15 \times 8¾ \times 5½$ inches. Now take the bottom piece, coat the edges with glue, and fit it into the box by setting the hollow box down over it, in the same manner as described for the wooden tackle box in Chapter 8. Drive three nails through each side and three through each end into the edges of the bottom piece to give extra strength to the bottom, since it will be carrying the weight of the shells. Countersink the finishing nails and fill the holes with plastic wood.

Using the diagram, plot the diagonal cuts and draw the ellipse that serves as the hand grip. The handle grip is made by drilling a ½-inch hole at one end of the ellipse, unhooking one end of the coping saw blade and passing it through the drilled hole, rehooking it, and then cutting around the ellipse so that it is removed in one piece.

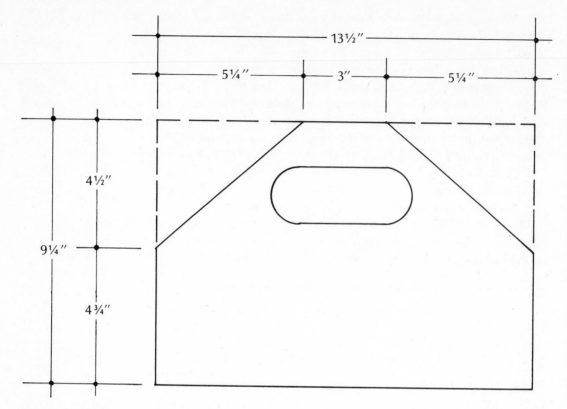

Detail of handle/divider.
See text for instructions on
how to make hole for
handle.

Now assemble the handle/divider into the center of the box. The easiest way to line it up properly is to take four boxes of shotgun shells and place them into the box, two on either side of the handle/divider. They will hold it in the proper position while it is nailed in place—three nails through each end, two through the bottom at each end where the wood contacts the bottom. And that's it; all you have to do now is sand it smooth and stain it.

The cut-out in the bottom-center of the handle/divider allows spent shell casings tossed into one side to roll through, so that there is more storage room; when a shell is spent, instead of loading up your shooting vest, just drop it in the box whenever you reach for a fresh shell; and at the end of the shooting session you have a place to store the 100 spent casings until you get a chance to reload them.

23
Shotshell Trimmer

Almost every rifle and pistol shooter in the country knows the importance of having cases all to the proper length, and that after repeated firings the brass cases tend to lengthen, and must therefore be trimmed back to factory length. Up to a certain point in stretch the expanded cases only affect accuracy. However, if the cases lengthen past a few thousandths of an inch, the neck can extend into the throat of the chamber and greatly increase pressures, even to the danger level.

Many shotgun enthusiasts fail to realize that their own shell cases are subject to linear expansion as well. I have often wondered how many shotgunners ever actually trim their cases. The new plastic cases greatly increase the number of times a shotshell can be reloaded, so there is an ever-greater chance of the shell stretching. If you have a few cases that have been reloaded say, six or more times, check the overall fired length with a pair of calipers. If they have expanded more than $1/32$ inch beyond the 2¾-inch standard, then they should be trimmed.

With the relatively low pressures generated by shotgun shells in modern steel chambers, there is not much danger of excess pressures, although that is always something to bear in mind. Rather, in the case of the shotgun, the case is designed to open up to its full size within the 2¾-inch chamber. If it exceeds this length, then the mouth extends partially into the forcing cone when it opens. Not only does this raise pressures, but it also plays havoc with the pattern, causing excessive stringing of the shot and deformed patterns. The case mouth in the forcing cone causes the wads to cock, and thereby allows gases to get past them and penetrate the shot column. This also results in a loss in velocity.

Shotshell trimmer is accurate and adaptable to different gauges.

If you shoot 3-inch chambers, you don't have to worry about this happening with the 2¾-inch shells, obviously, since a stretch of over ¼ inch would be readily noticeable when reloading. But you do have the problem with 3-inch shells in those same chambers, so it is a good idea to measure your cases after every third or fourth loading and firing.

Shotshell trimmers can be purchased. One sells for about $8.50 for one gauge, with extra adaptors ranging between $1 and $1.35, to trim all but 28-gauge shells. Another model for 12- or 20-gauge sells at approximately $6 apiece. As you can see, if you shoot a wide range of gauges, this can get pretty expensive. But you can make a trimmer that works perfectly, *plus* adaptors for all gauges, for 30 cents worth of materials and 30 minutes of your time. If you prefer, you can make separate trimmers for each gauge for about $1.25. I personally feel that, with the cost of materials so low, this is the best plan, because in anything that uses "adaptors" you are bound to lose a certain amount of accuracy.

This chapter explains in detail how to make an individual shotshell trimmer for the 12-gauge shell. Using this trimmer, and different sized dowels you can trim all but the 10-gauge shotshells; or, using the pattern and the dimensions given for the hole, dowel, and socket for each gauge, you can turn out individual trimmers for each of your gauges. All pieces of wood mentioned will be standard 1-inch white pine unless otherwise noted. Now, let's get to work.

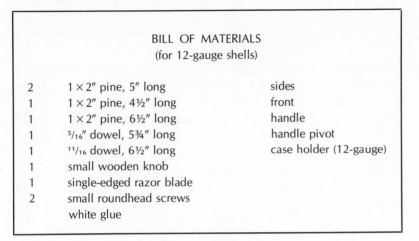

BILL OF MATERIALS
(for 12-gauge shells)

2	1 × 2″ pine, 5″ long	sides
1	1 × 2″ pine, 4½″ long	front
1	1 × 2″ pine, 6½″ long	handle
1	⁵/₁₆″ dowel, 5¾″ long	handle pivot
1	¹¹/₁₆ dowel, 6½″ long	case holder (12-gauge)
1	small wooden knob	
1	single-edged razor blade	
2	small roundhead screws	
	white glue	

DIMENSIONS OF CASE HOLDERS FOR OTHER GAUGES

Dowel size		Guide hole	Socket diameter
12 ga.	¹¹/₁₆″	¾″	⅞″
16 ga.	⅝″	¹¹/₁₆″	¹³/₁₆″
20 ga.	⁹/₁₆″	⅝″	¾″
28 ga.	⁷/₁₆″	½″	⅝″
.410	⅜″	⁷/₁₆″	⁹/₁₆″

The above measurements are based on the plastic case, which is the most commonly used today. However, I am well aware that many people still use the paper cases. The trimmer works even more easily on paper cases, but if using paper cases, decrease the dowel size and guide hole size by ¹/₁₆ inch to allow for extra thickness of the paper.

Pattern for shotshell trimmer handle.

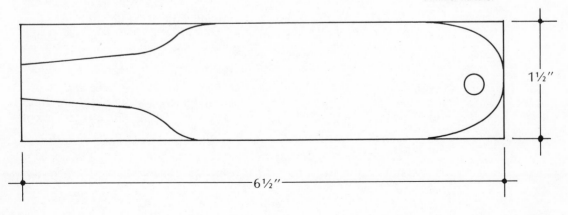

1½″

6½″

If you use a single length of 1×2, all you will need to worry about is the length of the pieces, since all other dimensions are the same as used. However, the "nose" form of the handle should be traced onto the wood to save estimation in trimming. Use the template so that all your trimmers will be of the same dimensions.

Once the pieces have been cut to size, take one of the 2×5-inch pieces, measure ½ inch from one end, and drill a ⁵⁄₁₆-inch hole centered in the width of the piece at that point. Now lay this piece atop the second piece of the same size, line up the edges, and, using that hole as a guide, drill through the second piece as well. Separate the pieces and, measuring 1½ inches back from the opposite end of one of them, drill a ¾-inch hole centered in the width of the board at that point, completely through the wood.

The next piece is a little more difficult to make, because it requires making a socket for the shotshell to ride in while it is being trimmed. However, with a little care it can be done perfectly on the first try.

Take the piece with the ¾-inch hole in it, and line it up with the other piece making certain that the two ⁵⁄₁₆-inch holes exactly coincide. Now, with a ¾-inch auger bit, slide the bit through the hole and *press* down into the wood of the second piece. Now separate the pieces again. The indentation made by the screw of the bit will provide the center for the socket hole. Now lay the piece with the indentation on the workbench, or on a scrap of lumber, but do not pin it down.

Use a brace and bit if at all possible; if you must use a power drill, use tape to make a depth gauge on the bit as you did with the no-danger reloading block (Chapter 18), ⅜ inch from the point of the drill. If you are using a brace and bit, the point of the screw on the end of the bit will determine the depth in the following manner. Use a ⅞-inch bit and, taking the indentation as center, start to drill very slowly. Due to the small size of the piece, you can lift the brace after every second turn, and the piece will come with it, so that you can look at the reverse side without having to back the bit out of the hole. Proceed in this manner until the point of the bit *just penetrates* the wood on the other side. Now back the bit out.

Remember, the bit for the brace has a long screw at the center; the bit for a power drill does not. If you are using the power drill, use the depth gauge, because if you should penetrate the piece completely, you'll have to start all over again. There is only one further operation to perform. One of the pieces you have just drilled should be lined up with the handle, so that the rounded end (not the tapered end) is flush with the end that has the ⁵⁄₁₆-inch hole. Put a pencil through that hole and mark the center on the handle. Separate the two pieces, and at that point on the handle drill a ⅜-inch hole through the handle. You are now ready to assemble the case trimmer and install the cutter blade.

Take the length of ⁵/₁₆-inch dowel, dip one end in white glue, and drive it into one of the ⁵/₁₆-inch holes. If you choose the side with the socket, make certain that the socket faces the same direction as the length of the dowel. Drive it through so that the end is flush with the opposite side of the wood.

Now take the 2 × 4½-inch piece, and nail it to the opposite end of the piece, extending in the same direction as the dowel. Slip the handle over the dowel. The larger hole assures a sliding fit. Make sure that the handle moves along the length of the dowel freely. If it does not, remove it and make the hole gradually larger until it slides easily along the dowel, but without wobbling. Now take the other side of the trimmer, the one with the ¾-inch hole, and drive it down over the dowel so that the front end comes flush with the front piece

Calibrating the dowel.

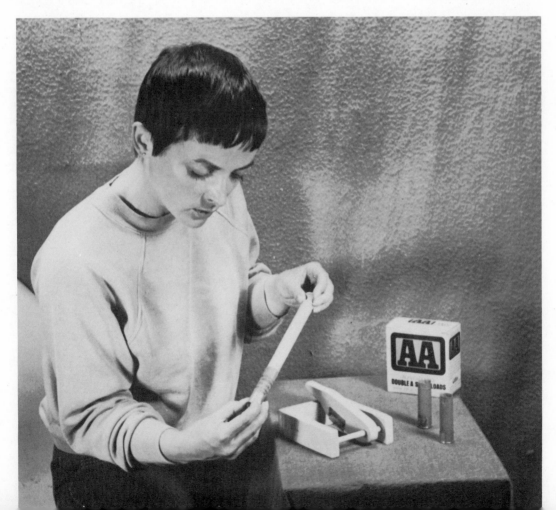

of the trimmer. Nail the front of the trimmer to the end of this side, and trim off any of the dowel which extends past the side.

Take the section of ¹¹/₁₆-inch dowel, and slide it through the ¾-inch hole so that the end rests in the socket. Let the handle down in contact with the dowel, and make a pencil mark on the handle at the point of contact. Using that mark as a guide, take a single-edged razor blade and screw it to the handle so that ⅛ inch of the blade extends down past the edge of the handle. Center the blade on the pencil mark, and screw it to the side of the handle which faces the socket of the trimmer.

The only other step is to calibrate the trimmer, by marking the ⁵/₁₆-inch dowel. Because of the socket, the very end of the dowel on the socket side measures ⅜ inch. Measure out from that side, and make a mark 2⅜ inches on the dowel. Make another mark ¼ inch from this mark, or 2⅝ inches from the socket side. These are the calibrations for trimming both 2¾- and 3-inch shells to factory length.

The trimmer is used in this manner. Turn the trimmer on its side so that the socket faces upwards. Set the base of a 12-gauge shell in the socket. Slide the large dowel through the hole in the opposite side of the trimmer, and into the shell as far as it will go. Now turn the trimmer back to the horizontal again. With the nose of the handle

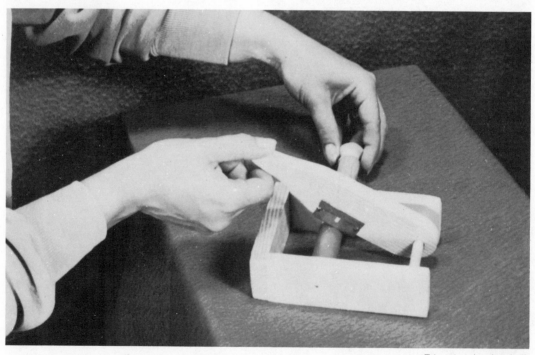

Trimming the shotshell.

facing you, and the shell toward your right, slide the handle toward the left until the 2¾-inch marking on the ⁵/₁₆-inch dowel is just visible. Bring the handle down so that the blade penetrates the shotshell case. Holding the handle down firmly, rotate the dowel a full 360 degrees. The blade will slice a perfect circle off the case, bringing it down to the required length.

There are some fine old European shotguns available on the used gun market which take 2½-inch shotshells, which are virtually unobtainable. Using this trimmer, and making another calibration on the dowel 2⅛ inches from the socket side, a person owning one of these guns can trim his regular cases to fit the odd-sized chamber.

Although the trimmer can be used with different-sized dowels to trim all the smaller gauges, it is more accurate to make a separate trimmer with the proper sized guide and socket. The chart of guide and socket sizes below the bill of materials makes the construction of several trimmers easier for the handy sportsman who shoots a wide variety of gauges, and reloads them all.

24

The Art
of the
Duck Decoy

Decoys are to the hunter what plugs are to the fisherman. Both are carvings, both are art forms in their own right, and both are, in effect, lures made of wood for the purpose of tricking game into striking distance of the sportsman. Just as an ill-formed or improperly balanced plug will fail to catch fish, an improperly balanced or constructed duck decoy will not only fail to lure the waterfowl within range, it will also eliminate any chances of their coming into range accidentally, since it will spook them away.

There is no way a chapter in a book of this sort can hope to deal with all the various methods of making duck decoys and painting them. The various decoys are entirely too numerous to deal with in anything short of a complete volume. Rather, this chapter will deal with the basic construction and painting techniques for two types of decoys. I hope that from that point you will develop an interest in one of the oldest crafts in the history of hunting, one which goes back to before the beginnings of recorded history. Decoys of sorts were being woven of straw, or manufactured of mud and sticks, by the American Indians when the first white explorers landed on these shores. From that time to the present the art of constructing and detailing duck decoys has been developed and refined, until today some decoy carvers are asking for and receiving up to $500 for a single carved decoy. The highest-priced decoys bear little resemblance to the commercial hunting models; the really expensive numbers have each feather outlined by the knife rather than just paint, and the painting itself is so meticulous that a person chancing upon one of these decoys sitting in a marsh would swear even at close range that it was a live duck. Naturally, such carving is the realm of the expert only, and has little bearing on the man who simply wants to make a string of decoys for his own use.

Both of the types discussed in this chapter are working decoys; that is, they are meant to be used in hunting. However, the second style, which involves more detailing, can also be used as a decoration in the home.

The first style of decoy is called a "block." This is the working decoy, and very seldom used as decoration, since it is relatively plain. In most cases, ducks will decoy to a set of blocks as readily as they will decoy to a set of highly detailed decoys, but in many instances the hunter himself feels more secure with the detailed paint jobs of the more difficult decoys. With this extra confidence in the decoys he allows the ducks to come in closer, and so his shooting is better—which goes to the credit of the detailed decoys. For actual efficiency, however, the plain blocks are just as effective as long as the hunter gives the ducks enough time to get within range.

BILL OF MATERIALS

For each decoy:

4	1 × 8″ pine, 18″ long	body
2	1 × 6″ pine, 6″ long	head
	⅜″ dowel	
	white glue	
	acrylic paints (see text)	

The methods involved in making the working decoy, or "block," are as follows: Cut four pieces of 1-inch pine or cedar to the size and shape shown in the illustration, and glue and clamp them as shown in the inset. Use a good-quality waterproof glue, and allow the decoys to remain under the clamps at least 24 hours to ensure the tightest bond possible.

Now take a mallet and chisel, and start cutting the edges off the step construction so that the block begins to take on a relatively rounded appearance. Go very slowly, working with the grain of the wood and taking off just a little at a time. If you try to hurry this step, or move against the grain, the chisel may well dig into the wood too deeply, and remove more than you wish. Remember, you can always shave more wood off the block, but this is one creation that you can't fill with plastic wood and have it look right if you gouge out too big a piece.

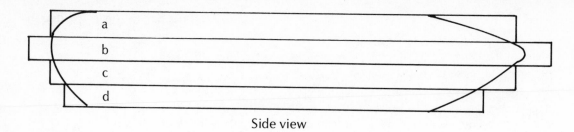

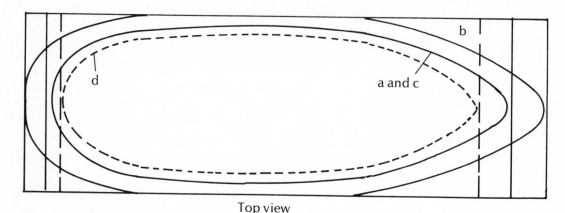

Side view

Top view

Pattern for body block. Top drawing shows a side view. Bottom drawing shows a top view. Carve along the curved lines. Pieces "a" and "c" are cut the same. Dotted line in lower drawing shows shape of "d". Scale is ⅓ actual size.

Once you have almost all of the "steps" shaved down with the mallet, go over the entire block with either the four-in-one wood rasp or the Surform tool to further round the body of the decoy. Make as smooth a curve as possible to the top of the block, while leaving the base of the block perfectly flat—although real ducks make out all right with their round bottoms in the water, I have never yet seen a round-bottomed decoy that rode the water correctly, especially if there is any wind. The flat-bottomed decoy will be far more stable and will not have the tendency to toss and roll that its more decorative cousin has, will be lighter in weight, and will be easier to fit up with decoy hardware.

A photograph of the "steps", described above.

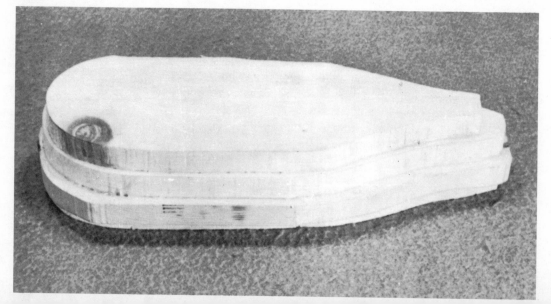

After you have made the curve of the body as smooth as possible with the rasp, go over it first with coarse and then with medium sandpaper to take the tool marks out of the wood. Don't use fine sandpaper or steel wool, however, since a little roughness is desirable on these working blocks, for two reasons. First, the roughness allows the paint to adhere better; second, the roughness eliminates the possibility of a high gloss paint job, and I know from personal experience that high gloss paint on a decoy will keep the ducks away more efficiently than a completely unpainted block.

You can, of course, carve the body from a solid block of wood, measuring a true $6 \times 7\frac{1}{2} \times 18$ inches. The next two illustrations show such a decoy. However, you will not be able to get soft pine in these dimensions; you should use cedar.

Now file part of the decoy flat again. It seems like a lot of extra work, but it makes a better and more natural-looking job if you round the block first. Take the flat side of the four-in-one rasp and flatten the section at the front of the block, shown in the illustration. This flat will provide a mount to fasten the head of the decoy. Although some decoy makers leave the body rounded and then attempt to cut the base of the neck of the decoy head to fit the rounded area, such a method is far more difficult, time-consuming, and unnecessary to both the finished appearance and efficacy of the decoy.

Now glue two pieces of 1-inch pine together with clamps, and lay out the pattern for the head on them after they are dry. You can glue and clamp several pieces overnight so that you can make several heads at a time. If you don't have enough clamps, you can accomplish the same end by nailing the pieces together through the waste wood on the outside of the head, in the area which will be cut away from the head.

You may wonder at the withdrawn necks of these patterns if you have not worked decoys before. The duck swims with its head withdrawn when it is relaxed, and with its neck extended and erect if something has alarmed or bothered it. Naturally, more ducks will come in to a set-up of relaxed and peaceful appearing decoys than will come to a lay-out that looks as though they are about to take off at any moment. You may also be wondering at the extra work involved in gluing two pieces of 1-inch pine together when you could use a single piece of 2-inch lumber. 2-inch lumber tends to have a rougher, more open grain, which does not shape as well, and which is harder to seal against the elements. In addition, the strip of glue down the middle of the head will strengthen the head, especially in the bill area. This is the most fragile part of the decoy and the section

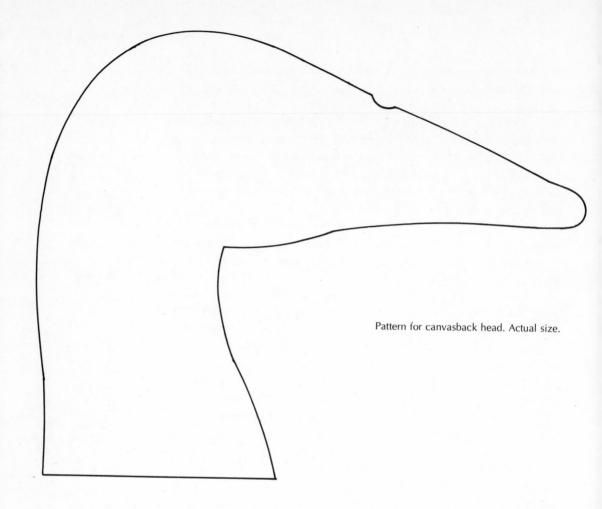

Pattern for canvasback head. Actual size.

most prone to breakage with incautious handling—ducks have a disconcerting tendency of flaring away from decoys without beaks.

Cut the pattern for the head out of the wood with a coping saw, and carve the head to a smoothly rounded shape in the same manner described for making plugs (Chapter 12). The smoothness of the head is important, since it cannot be blocky or squared at all; in fact, the heads for these simple blocks and the heads for the decorative decoys should be made in the same manner, although the painting does not have to be as detailed on the heads for the blocks as it does for the others. The heads should be no smoother than the bodies, since the early morning sun shining brightly on a glossy decoy's head will spook the ducks.

Once the head is smoothed, drill a ⅜-inch hole into the bottom of the head and insert a length of dowel. Cut the dowel off so that it extends 2 inches past the base of the neck. Position the head over the flat section on the body, and make a mark where the dowel touches the body. One of the easiest ways of doing this is to dip the end of the dowel in either lamp black or dark carpenter's chalk; it will then leave its own mark when it is brought in contact with the body. Now drill a ⅜-inch hole 2 inches deep at the point of contact.

Remove the dowel from the neck of the decoy, and coat both the dowel and the base of the decoy neck with waterproof glue. Reinsert one end of the dowel into the hole in the neck, and the other end into the hole in the body, and shove the head down firmly against the block. The dowel will strengthen and reinforce the head so that it will not be affected by a slight blow to the side, which might otherwise break off a head that was simply butt glued to the body.

The decoy keels can be made, but they can be purchased so cheaply that there is little point in making them. If you insist on making the entire thing yourself, the easiest way of making the keel is to purchase bar solder, drill three holes through a length sufficient to the size of the decoy, and mount it to the bottom with brass wood screws.

To make the decoy ride naturally in the water (even with the flat base the decoy will have a tendency to pitch in waves without a keel), attach the keel in the following manner. Take two heavy rubber bands and stretch them over the body of the decoy. Slip the keel through them, under the decoy, and place the decoy in a filled bathtub. Now, rock it from side to side. If it always returns to sit properly, take it out of the water and screw the keel to the base. If it does not return to the proper position, move the keel around under the rubber bands until it does, and then affix the keel firmly. The rubber bands enable you to make adjustments without screwing and unscrewing the weight. This method was taught to me by an old duck hunter who was renowned throughout the Chesapeake Bay area: he never once failed to bag his limit. He claimed that he owed his success solely to his decoys, and that may have been true, since he never used a call, and was possessed of a habit that was very disconcerting to anyone gunning with him. Raised during the Depression, he was very chary with his shotgun shells, and would hold back his shooting until two ducks crossed, so that he could drop them both with one shot.

All right, now you are ready to paint the block. Refer to the illustration for the proper pattern. Remember this is a working decoy and need not be detailed to the point of painting in individual feathers; save that for the decorative type. However, the colors used and the general pattern do have to be right. For the purpose of simplicity on this first block, we will make a canvasback representation.

In painting these decoys, both the plain blocks and the decorative models, use either acrylic artist's colors or flat latex housepaint. DO NOT use oil paints or enamels, for the same reasons that you do not sand the decoy perfectly smooth—the high gloss of the oil bases will cause the decoys to shine and cast reflections in the water, and they will scare the incoming ducks away. I strongly recommend the acrylics over housepaint, since they seem to bond better, are quite reasonable in cost, and they enable you to purchase more of the necessary colors for the detailing on the decorative decoys.

Assuming that you have used the canvasback head and the decoy is now ready for painting, apply an overall coat of white to the block, head and all. This is a base coat to seal the wood, and for this base coat you can use housepaint if you wish, since base coats on several dozen blocks would involve quite a few tubes of artist's colors. After the white has dried, make a very thin wash of pale gray and go over the body of the decoy. You will find some instructions that recommend leaving the body pure white, and certainly this looks prettier to the hunter, but the body of a canvasback is not the snow white hue that the pure white pigment would imply. The pale gray wash mutes the brilliance of the white, but not enough to give the appearance of a gray duck, so make the wash as thin as possible while still retaining a little of the gray pigment.

The chest, tail, and the feathers under the tail are pure Mars Black straight from the tube. For some reason black pigment, no matter what

Prime the decoy with white paint.

Once the main colors are blocked in, the working decoy is finished.

form of paint it comes in, takes longer to dry than any other pigment (white seems to dry the fastest) so allow plenty of time for this to dry before painting the head.

The head looks like a brick; that's about the best way of describing the color, which is much less intense than the red head of the Redhead. Mix equal parts of Burnt Sienna and Burnt Umber, with a little white mixed in thoroughly in order to lighten the intensity and darkness of the two pigments, and add a small touch of Yellow Ochre. Paint the head and neck all the way down to the body, and then paint the bill black. The eyes are Cadmium Red Light with a black pupil and black rim. I have seen many blocks that don't even utilize eyes, since by the time the ducks get close enough to see the eyes of the decoy they are supposed to be well within range, but that far I won't go. Put on eyes. Whether or not it makes any difference to the ducks, it will probably make you feel better and give you enough confidence to let the ducks get those few yards further in that can mean the difference between a sky-busting miss and a roast duck dinner.

Decorative decoys usually require more elaborate carving and fine detail painted and/or carved in.

The decorative type of decoy, now that the block is finished, can also be used as a working decoy if you like, since it is constructed in much the same manner, but, being much prettier, it can also be used as a house decoration—either by itself or as the base for a lamp, or whatever. In making the decorative decoy add two more pieces of 1-inch pine to the bottom (see illustration) and carve them so that the belly of the decoy is rounded as well as its back. Proceed in the same manner as for the block, only when you come to the sanding, go the full route through 220 grit garnet paper.

After the decoy is sanded smoothly, take a hobby knife or X-acto knive and, making small V-cuts, accentuate the separation of the bill from the head, and the dip between and beneath the folded wings. If you are really going all out you can delineate separate feathers.

In this type of decoy, the eyes are more important, since you will be staring into them whatever you do with the duck. Although they can be painted on, as in the case of the mallard shown in the illustration, it is even better to use the small glass eyes sold by many taxidermist's supply shops. These eyes have flat backs, and are joined together with a small wire. To apply them, drill two tiny holes in the sides of the head, snip the wire in the middle, and apply glue to the back of the eye. Then force the wire into the hole, and the eyes are all set. The eyes cost about $1.50 for 12 pair at the time of this writing, and since they make a much better job than painted eyes for decorative decoys, they are a worthwhile investment. Some of the better supply houses sell eyes that are the specific colors of the birds you are trying to duplicate.

The finished decorative decoy in the illustration is a mallard. A list of colors required to paint it follows. Because so little of one color is required on a single decoy in many cases, I have made up a list that will cover a total of 24 decoys. Remember that the same colors will be used in blocks; the major difference will be in the amount of brush work. The diagram which accompanies this chapter shows the decoy and the locations for the various colors. Here is the list:

yellow ochre:	1 ounce	(bill)
metallic green:	4 ounces	(head)
burnt sienna:	8 ounces	(wing primaries)
medium gray:	8 ounces	(sides)
dark gray:	4 ounces	(secondary feathers)
light gray:	4 ounces	(feather detailing)
pthalo blue:	1 ounce	(wing feathers)
black:	4 ounces	(rump, feather detailing)
white:	1 ounce	(tip of tail, neck ring, feather details)
light brown:	16 ounces	(wings and back)

Making decoys is a little like making fishing plugs or tying flies, not only in the sort of creative work involved, but also in the tremendous satisfaction that comes when you see that massive flock of ducks or gaggle of geese make a sweeping turn in the sky and come in toward the blind, fooled by a decoy you made with your own two hands. And the variety is endless; you can make as many decoys as you wish, and of every species you are likely to run across; in fact, you can even use pictures from bird books to make decorative decoys of foreign birds, and of species now extinct or protected by law. You can also diversify and carve shorebirds and other gamebirds as well; and, as in the making of plugs, you can either go all out and manufacture a great number as a massive project; or, you can settle for making just a few of different species as decorations for the house, cutting out the rough forms in the garage and putting the finishing touches on them in front of a roaring fire while a cold February wind wails outside the house. Either way, decoy making is a hobby which, once begun, is not easily put aside.

25
Silhouette
Dove Decoys

Ducks are not the only game lured by decoys. Crows are easily decoyed with a stuffed owl or effigies of other crows, or even dead crows hung in trees. But not many people realize that doves can be decoyed as well, and that, when the doves are flying high and fast, a set of decoys may be the only method of drawing them close enough for a shot.

The easiest sort of dove decoys to make are of the silhouette variety, cut from a sheet of ¼-inch plywood. I have never been able to understand why they work so well, and I have always wondered what the living mourning dove thinks when it flies over the top of the decoys and they disappear. But I do know that the silhouette decoys work, and they are easy to make and use, and eminently portable.

BILL OF MATERIALS

For each decoy:

1	9 × 12 × ¼" plywood	
	flat gray paint	
1	wire coat hanger	
1	screw eye	
OR		
1	9 × 12 × ¼" corrugated cardboard	body
1	4 × 6 × ¼" corrugated cardboard	wings
	flat gray paint	
1	wire coat hanger	
1	screw eye	

To save you trouble, a full-size diagram is included which you can lay over carbon paper, and trace the form directly onto the plywood. They are very economical, as two dozen decoys can be made from a single 2 × 4-foot sheet of plywood. Cut out the forms with a coping saw, sand the edges to remove burrs and splinters, and paint them a light grayish brown. If you are exceptionally particular, you can get a color photograph or painting of a mourning dove, carry it to the paint store, and match it as closely as possible from their photographs of paint colors or their color chips. This degree of exactness is unnecessary. Any medium shade of gray will suffice quite nicely, so long as it is not too intense. As with the duck decoys, however, make certain that the paint is of the latex flat variety, because most dove shooting is done on relatively sunny days, and the sun glinting off a brightly shining decoy (which disappears when the doves pass over it) is more than likely to drive them to the next hunter down the field. Only fish, amphibians, and some reptiles actually have a reflective sheen.

Now install a screw eye at the point marked "X" on the diagram. Cut up some coat hangers, and bend 4-inch sections of the wire into "S" shaped hooks, as many as you need for the number of decoys you are making. With a magic marker, outline the wings, color the beak, and draw in an eye.

You will need one of your fishing rods to place the decoys. Here's how it is done. Hook one loop of the "S" hook through the screw eye, and hang the other end through the tip guide on the fishing rod. Now reach up into a tree with the rod, hook the wire over a branch, and pull the rod back to you. The decoy will remain hung on the branch until it is removed in the reverse manner.

Another method of placing these decoys, although not quite as effective as the tree-mounted decoys, is nevertheless effective at times, particularly in areas with no trees. The same decoys can be used as stick-ups, by simply boring an ⅛-inch hole in the lower edge of the plywood and inserting a 6-inch length of coat-hanger wire. Make some of the holes directly at the bottom, and some more toward the breast, so that the flocks of decoys will resemble a real flock (of flat doves), with some erect and others leaning forward in a feeding position.

These decoys, especially the ground models, can also be made of corrugated cardboard, which will be even lighter than the wood silhouettes. With cardboard models you can cut out wings (see diagram) and, by slotting the cardboard body as well as the wings, you

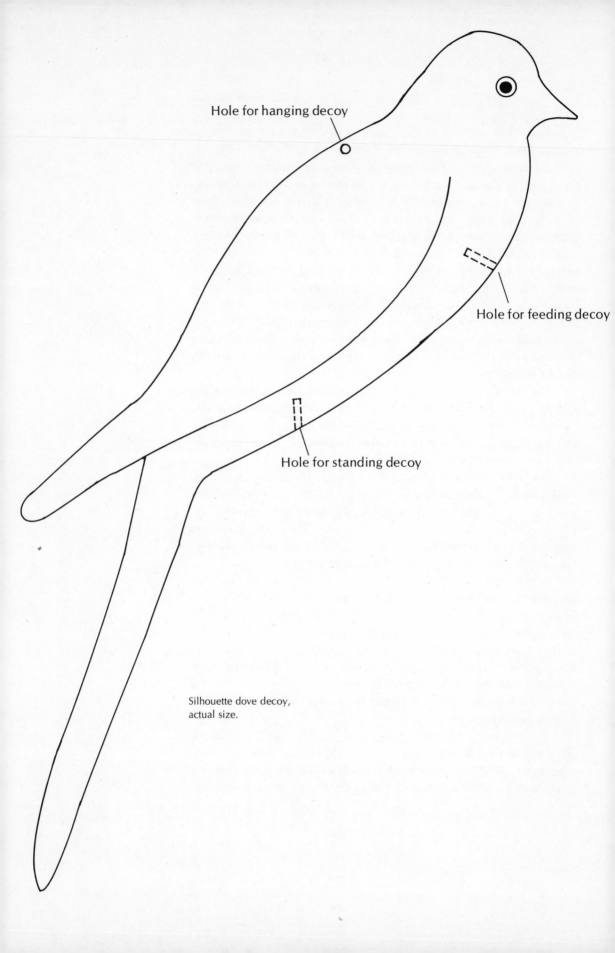

Hole for hanging decoy

Hole for feeding decoy

Hole for standing decoy

Silhouette dove decoy,
actual size.

The silhouettes hang suspended by hooks made of bent coat hangers.

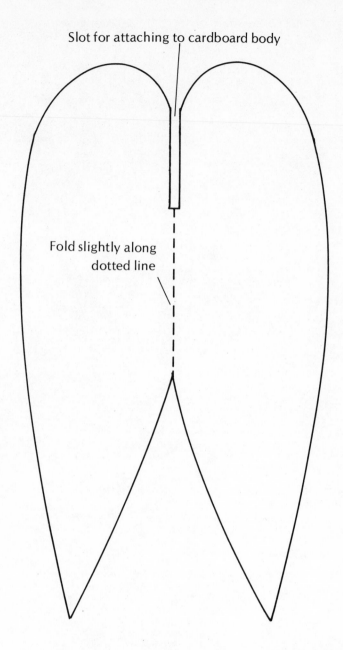

Slot for attaching to cardboard body

Fold slightly along
dotted line

Wing template for card-
board dove decoys.

can approximate a three-dimensional decoy. Again, paint the whole decoy gray, and make sure that the house paint fills the holes around the edges of the cardboard. I doubt that a dove could see the corrugations, or that a perforated dove would look less friendly than a normal flat dove, but in the event of a sudden shower the water won't get into the inside of the corrugations and destroy your decoys as quickly.

You can fashion two other types of decoys. You can make three-dimensional wood models using the template provided and referring

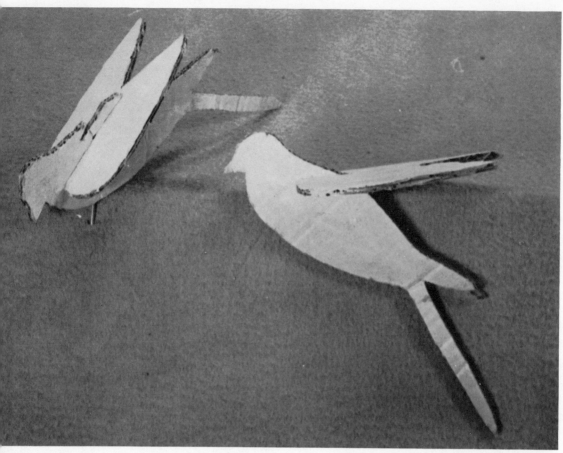

to Chapter 24 for instructions. These really look good, and will last practically forever. However, they are time-consuming to make, they cost far more than the silhouettes, and they are heavy to carry, especially if you want a good spread. They may be slightly better on the ground than even the silhouettes with wings.

Alternatively, if you want to experiment with three-dimensional dove decoys at less expense and weight, try making a few from papier mâché. Use the same basic pattern, and squeeze plaster-coated wet paper into the general shape. Then cover smoothly with strips of the papier mâché to make a more natural appearing bird. Let dry, varnish, and paint flat pale gray. Don't use water base paint first, because the paint might saturate the papier mâché and your decoy will end up looking lumpy. Spray varnish will seal the decoy for the paint, and will also help preserve the decoys from showers.

The papier mâché decoys, as with all the others, have certain advantages and certain disadvantages. They look "realer," particularly in ground sets, than the silhouette decoys. They take less time to make and are both cheaper and lighter than the three-dimensional wooden dove decoys. On the other hand, they are still bulky (eight silhouette decoys can be carried in the same space as one three-dimensional one), and the papier mâché is more prone to damage than wood.

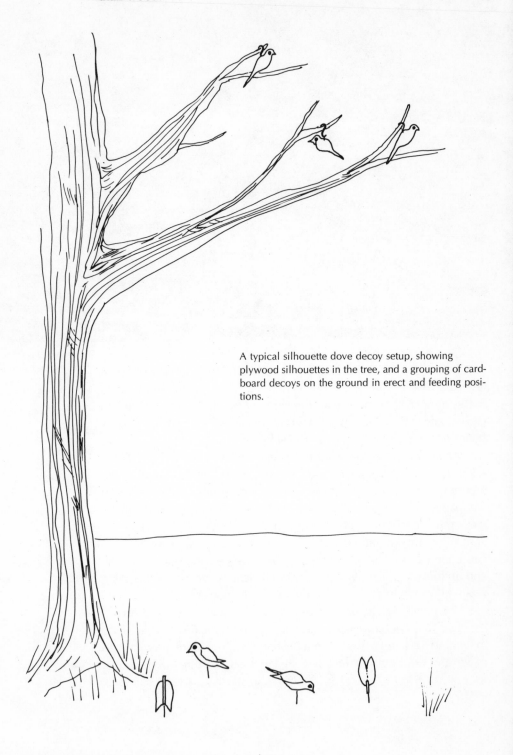

A typical silhouette dove decoy setup, showing plywood silhouettes in the tree, and a grouping of cardboard decoys on the ground in erect and feeding positions.

26
Squirrel Call

The squirrel, in all of its various subspecies, is probably the most popular of all American small game. It is prolific, it is found almost everywhere, and bag limits are very liberal. It can be taken with the .22, with shotgun, with handgun, with bow and arrow, and with reduced loads in a high-powered rifle. It is most likely the first game that a hunter kills, and in many cases if you ask a man what got him started on hunting, he will tell you it was his first squirrel when he was a boy. Stalking squirrels through dry autumn woods is excellent practice for big-game hunts, since squirrels will spook at the slightest untoward sound.

Hunting squirrels requires little equipment except a gun and patience, but there are many times, especially when you know a squirrel is on the opposite side of a tree, that a squirrel call helps by arousing the game's curiosity and making it peek around the tree. The most commonly used call is the bellows type; second in popularity is the box-and-striker. The bellows call requires a special rubber bellows and a reed installed on a hollowed wooden tube; leave the construction of these to the major call manufacturers. The box and striker can easily be manufactured right in your own home, for about half the cost of a purchased model.

BILL OF MATERIALS

1	1 × 2 × 4" cedar (or hardwood)	body
1	¹/₁₆ × 1¼ × 3" marine brass	strike plate
2	½" round headed brass wood screws	
1	20d common nail	striker
	marine varnish	

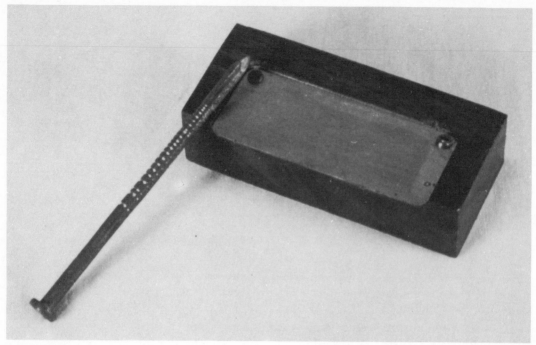

Box-and-striker type squirrel call.

If you live near a boat yard, you may be able to beg everything you need. Ask the owner if you can look through his trash barrels at the end of the day. Scraps of brass are often thrown out that are too small for marine use, but large enough for our purposes. You may even be able to find a piece of walnut or mahogany to use in place of the cedar. If you don't have a boat yard near you, all the pieces required can be found in most good hobby shops for less than $1.

Take the block of wood and lay it out as shown in the diagram. Carve out the recess as shown with a pocket knife or a chisel. Now give the block four coats of marine varnish, but do not get any of the varnish in the recess, which is the sounding box of the call. You may find in carving the recess that the hardwood is too difficult to work with a pocketknife unless you are experienced with whittling and carving. Since the sounding box does have to be made well in order to get the proper tone from the call, you will be better off using a mallet and chisel. Draw the outline of the cut-out onto the wood and, aligning the flat (rather than the beveled) side of the chisel with the outside of the call, strike the hilt of the chisel lightly with the mallet, so that the chisel cuts straight down into the wood. Be especially careful when making the cut along the rear edge of the call, since you will be striking with the grain and an overly hard tap can split the wood completely.

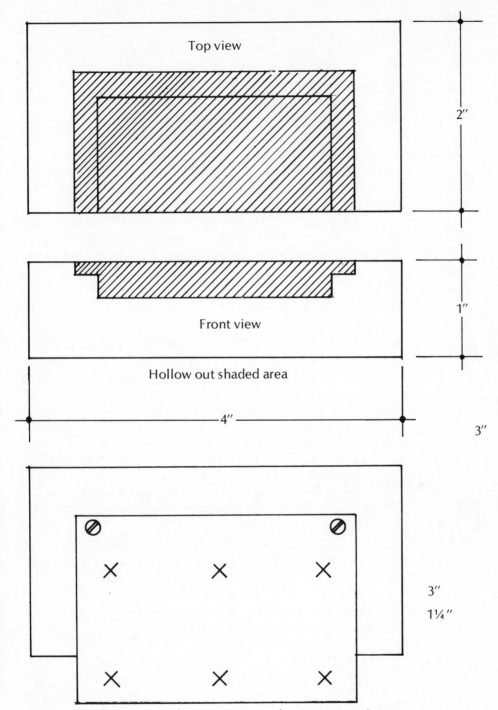

Top view

2"

Front view

1"

Hollow out shaded area

4"

3"

3"

1¼"

Mount brass plate as shown. "X"s mark pressure point to modulate call.

Construction diagram of call box.

The cuts in the wood will now look like those shown in the illustration—a half-V with the slope on the inside edge of the cut. Now place the call in a vise, and begin removing the excess wood from the sound box. If your chisel is sharp enough, you should be able to accomplish this task by shoving the chisel by hand; if it isn't, you will have to use the mallet again. If you do, remove the wood with very, very light taps and very shallow cuts, since too much force too near the ends will split those ends right off the call and you'll have to start all over again. Work gradually, from the outer edges to the center, removing just a little wood at a time. Once most of the wood is removed finish smoothing the bottom of the recess with a scraping motion of the chisel. Finish it off with sandpaper, although the recess does not have to be perfectly smooth. Then apply the varnish to the outside of the call and mount the brass piece over the recess as shown with the two brass screws. You are now ready to make the striker.

Take the 20d nail, and, using a triangular file, cut grooves all the way around the nail, for 3 inches of its length. This takes some time, but have patience. The grooves only have to be about $1/32$ inch deep.

That's all there is to it. To call squirrels, draw the striker across the edge of the brass plate two or three times, lightly, for its full length. Follow this with three or four short strokes. Keep the strokes short and light and fast, and pause about 5 seconds between each series. You will notice in the diagram a series of six "p"'s on the striker plate. If you press your thumb at any of these points, you can alter the tone of the call. Practice at the various positions, and you will be able to change the tone to fit the voices of the squirrels in your area.

27

Turkey Call

If you made the squirrel call and liked the sound of it, here is another call, slightly more difficult to make, that has proved its effectiveness for many, many years. Don't worry about the efficacy of a home-made turkey call; when they were first developed by mountaineers, they were all hand-carved, and the mountaineers have probably killed more turkeys than every other hunter put together.

Many hunters use the diaphragm variety of call that fits in the mouth. This has certain advantages, as it leaves both hands free to handle the gun quickly, and, since the hands aren't moving at all, with the only motion being the slight movement of the lips, there is nothing to startle the turkey. I, however, will never use a diaphragm call again. Six years ago I was on a turkey stand in Western Maryland. It was my first trip for turkey. I had practiced with the call until I was in danger from male turkeys, but since I figured that the shot would get to them before they could creep up behind me, I worked at the call with great fervor. Almost immediately, I started getting an answer, and when the tom showed up, it was the biggest damned bird I had ever seen in my life. In my astonishment, I gulped. Two days later I started practicing with the chalked box, and have been using it ever since.

This call is made out of hardwood, and there are no substitutions. Softwood and plywood simply do not have the tone. Get either

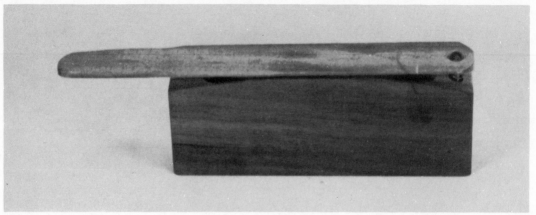

Hand-held turkey call.

maple or ash, and purchase it at a hobby wood store rather than a lumber yard. You can get smaller pieces there, and with the price of good hardwood there is no sense in purchasing any more than you have to. You can buy thin pieces of wood in the hobby wood stores as well, and this will save you the problem of attempting to plane the sides down to the proper thickness.

BILL OF MATERIALS		
2	⅛ × 2¼ × 7″ hardwood	sides
1	1½ × 2 × 7″ hardwood	body of call
1	½ × 2 × 9″ hardwood	paddle striker
1	No. 6 × 1″ roundhead brass screw	
1	weak compression spring, 1″ long, to slide over shank of screw	
	glue	
1	piece of chalk	

The only tools necessary for its construction are a coping saw, a rather fine file, sandpaper, and a drill.

Refer to the pattern for the proper way of cutting the block, which forms the ends, bottom, and sounding box of the call. This is a simple cut made with the coping saw, and goes all the way through the block. Don't think that you can save on wood by purchasing thinner pieces and gluing them together—the sound won't be the same.

Now take the two 7-inch pieces of ⅛-inch stock and glue them to the sides of the body, making certain that the bottom edge of each

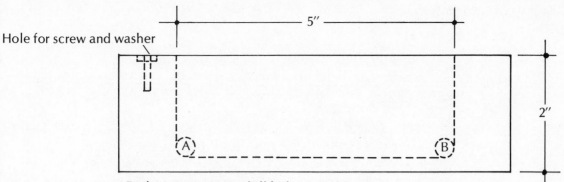

Hole for screw and washer

Body construction: drill holes A and B, cut out rest along dotted
lines with coping saw.

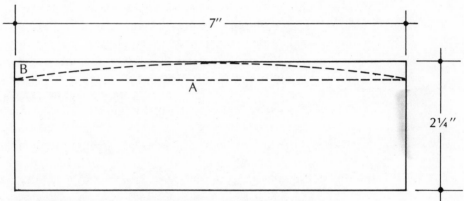

Dotted line A shows top of body in relation to sides.
Dotted line B shows curve to be made on thin sides of call.

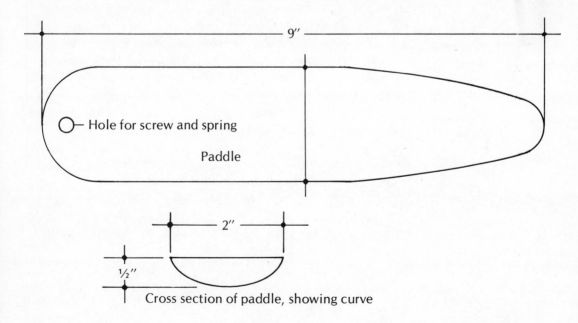

Hole for screw and spring

Paddle

Cross section of paddle, showing curve

Construction details for turkey call.

piece is flush with the edge of the body. You may be tempted to use brads to affix the sides to the body as well as the glue. DON'T! The pure tone comes from the vibrations of the wood when chalked and stroked, and the tone is slightly different if the brads compress the grain of the wood.

After the glue has dried you will have a box, the sides of which protrude ¼ inch above the main, hollowed-out body block. With either a compass, ruler, or dividers, whichever you happen to have, locate the exact center of the protruding edge, and mark it. Using that mark as the apex of an arc, taper the upper edges of the sides so that they slope in a curve from a point ¼ inch above the main body in the center to flush with the body ends, so that it looks like figure B in the illustration. Use a fine wood file and sandpaper to do this, slowly, so as not to split the wood or remove too much. Remember that the side extensions must have an even curve, so make the arc with a compass and follow the line closely—bumps or dips in the edge will eliminate the possibility of accurate sound from the call.

With the coping saw, cut the remaining piece of hardwood to the shape shown in the diagram. This will be the striker of the box. Now move back 3 inches from the handle end, and remove half the thickness of the paddle from this point out to the end of the handle. With the file and sandpaper, taper the body of the paddle into a smooth curve, running from a very thin edge along the sides to full thickness along the center line.

Now drill a ¼-inch hole through the end of the paddle marked X, and a ⅛-inch pilot hole for the screw, ½ inch deep, where marked on the diagram of the body. Drill a $5/16$-inch diameter depression, ¼ inch deep, at the same place, using the pilot hole as the center for the larger hole. This larger hole will retain the compression spring, which should be no stronger than those used in ball-point pens, although of greater diameter. Insert one end of the spring in the depression, slip the brass screw through the hole in the end of the paddle, and screw it into the body of the block through the spring. The pilot hole serves both to center the screw and to keep the body of the call from splitting. The compression spring exerts just enough pressure on the paddle to keep it from wobbling back and forth like a see-saw, thus allowing consistency in the tone of the call. By turning the screw in or out slightly, the tone may be adjusted. Make certain that the paddle pivots loosely on the screw and spring—if there is any friction on the screw, remove it and slightly enlarge the hole in the paddle.

The call should now be sanded with 220 grit garnet paper to make all surfaces smooth and slightly round all sharp corners. The call is now ready to use. Take a piece of chalk and chalk up the rounded under-surface of the paddle. When it is stroked back and forth against the curved sides, it sounds like a turkey gobble. With practice you can really call them in.

28

Crow Call

This crow call uses a reed, just like the commercial calls available in stores for between $3 and $10. While the tone may not be quite up to the commercial variety, I can vouch for the fact that it does, indeed, attract crows.

	BILL OF MATERIALS	
1	1¼" seasoned dowel, 3½" long	barrel
1	½" seasoned dowel, 2½" long	mouthpiece
1	.01 sheet brass, ½ × 1½"	reed

The first step is to make the barrel of the call, which is also the sound box. Make this out of 1¼-inch dowel. The outside diameter is not crucial, and if it is over or under by ⅛ to ¼ inch, don't worry about it. A very rustic-looking call can be made from a tree branch of approximately that diameter, simply by removing the bark. You must, however, find a dead, solid branch. Green wood will split and change tone as it dries out. So the best bet is to use a seasoned dowel for your first attempt. It will last longer.

Cut the dowel to a 3½-inch length, and drill a ½-inch hole lengthwise through the center. Now cut a 2½-inch length of ½-inch dowel, and drill a ¼-inch hole through the center. Take the drilled ½-inch dowel, and with the coping saw cut it very carefully in half, lengthwise. Now, with a file, start 1 inch from the end on the flat portion of the split dowel, and taper both pieces toward the end so that the very end is only ⅛ inch thick. When the two dowels are put together again, there will be a V-shaped notch between them.

Crow calls, commercial
and home made.

The reed is made from relatively stiff plastic or thin sheet metal. Go to a hobby store, the kind that sells materials for making models, and get a piece of sheet brass measuring .01 thick. On the brass, draw a slightly sized-up silhouette of the mouthpiece, and cut it out. This is the reed. Smooth the edges with very fine emery paper. Place the reed between the two halves of the ½-inch dowel, and install in the barrel of the call with a friction fit. Using a light mallet or another piece of wood, tap this mouthpiece in very lightly, checking the sound after each tap until you get the proper pitch with little vibration. If the call is too harsh, rub the wood thoroughly with linseed oil, which will mellow the tone. Apply the oil only to the barrel.

Now go talk to some crows.

29

Shooter's Bipod

As every varmint hunter who uses a high-powered, long-range rifle well knows, the most important thing is steadiness. 1½ M.O.A. becomes a 9-inch group at 600 yards, and no matter how effective the cartridge is at long ranges, a ½-inch miss is less effective than throwing a rock, because a ½-inch miss is still a miss, while you might hit the critter with a rock.

A tripod is the steadiest support short of welding the gun to the roof of your Land Rover and aiming the car rather than the gun, but when you put a bipod on a gun, you have a tripod in effect, with your body making the third leg.

Several varieties of home-made bipods work well. They are all quite simple, so I present them all briefly. Choose the one which suits you best.

BILL OF MATERIALS

scrap lumber, either 1" pine or ¾" marine plywood
½" dowels, sharpened in pencil sharpener
inner tube, felt, glue

Most important, a bipod must be steady. It must either provide a very sturdy rest when the gun is laid across the top of it, or it must affix to the gun in such a manner that the shooter himself makes the third leg of a tripod.

One of the easiest ways of making the bipod requires almost no construction on your part, at least if you are a photographer. If you happen to have an old, small tripod (the very low, travelling variety) lying around collecting dust, you can use it in one of two ways. The first method involves removing the camera screw from the tripod plate and, using a wood screw, attaching a curved piece of wood, as shown in the drawing, to serve as a gun cradle. This is quite steady, and can be readily adjusted for both prone and sitting positions.

Or, the tripod can be attached to the gun itself. This makes a much steadier rest, since the tripod actually holds the gun in position. Of course it would be extremely awkward to carry, so there must be a way of both attaching and removing the tripod rather easily. All tripods carry a standard ¼ × 20 thread camera screw. At the local hardware store, buy a nut that will fit the ¼ × 20 thread. Drill a slight depression in the bottom of the forearm of your varmint gun, and epoxy the nut in place. (Take care with the epoxy cement, however; if it gets on the inside of the threads of the nut you won't be able to screw the tripod to the gun, and the chemicals involved in epoxy cements may damage the finish on some guns.) The tripod can then be carried on your belt, and screwed into either gun or camera at any moment.

If you don't have a tripod, you can still make some quite serviceable bipods very inexpensively. For example, the one shown in illustration A, a one-piece construction, can be cut from either 1-inch pine (nominal) or ¾-inch marine plywood. I prefer the plywood—there is less chance of stress against grain causing the bipod to break at a crucial moment. The one variable, the size of the hole, is determined by the outside diameter of your particular gun barrel. Measure the barrel directly forward of the forearm with calipers, and go directly by the measurement. Sand the bipod very smooth, and glue a strip of heavy felt around the inside of the hole. The felt protects the finish of the barrel, and provides a friction fit so that the bipod won't slip around the gun. The hole, as you will notice from the illustration, is located near the top of the bipod to provide clearance for the scope sights—there is nothing more disconcerting than looking through your varmint scope and having a 20× magnified view of the top of your bipod.

This bipod, as well as the monopod described later on, can have the legs affixed in a different manner. Instead of cutting out the legs integrally with the barrel band of the bipod, drill two holes into the outside of the circle that will form the barrel band, and insert ⅜-inch dowels approximately 6–8 inches long. Glue them in, and when the glue has dried, sharpen the protruding ends in a pencil sharpener. Dowels, being straight-grained hardwood, will very seldom break and the pointed ends are excellent, especially in farm fields when going after wary 'chucks.

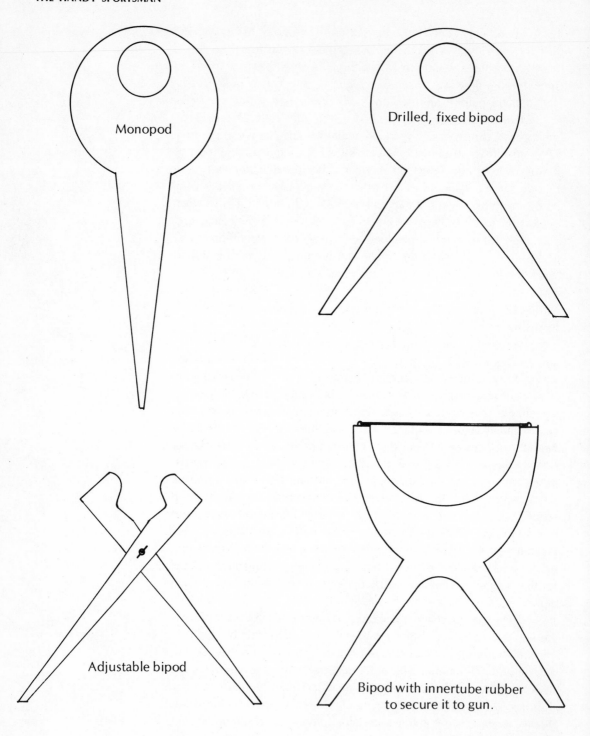

Monopod

Drilled, fixed bipod

Adjustable bipod

Bipod with innertube rubber
to secure it to gun.

Patterns for variety of bipods and a monopod.

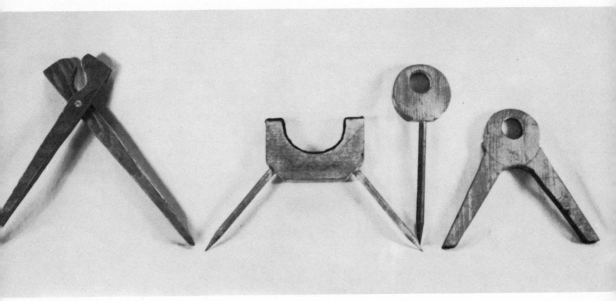

Make them as carefully as you want; these are crude but serviceable.

The second type of bipod is the scissors variety. The two legs are made to the same pattern as shown in illustration B; one is then reversed and the two are fitted together with a carriage bolt and wing nut as shown. Line the upper arms of the scissors with felt, and glue two strips of coarse emery cloth to the inside of the joint so that the rough sides meet to provide a gripping surface. Install a lock washer under the wing nut. Although the gun barrel can pivot and cant in this variety it is still pretty steady. This bipod can adapt to gun barrels of any diameter, or to rifles with full-length tubular magazines.

The third and final variety also has a friction fit like the first, but is made with a piece of inner tube stretched across the top. In making the wood form, use the same pattern as that described and illustrated for the gun cradle on the tripod. Attach the inner tube strip to the top of the bipod with a washer on either side of the inner tube, between it and both the wood and the screw, to protect the rubber from being torn by the screw. This bipod adapts itself to various gun barrel diameters. However, it is not as effective on the tubular-magazine varieties such as the Winchester Model 9422M, because the tension of the inner tube has a tendency to pivot the barrel on its magazine, pulling it sideways and canting the gun. Once again, as with all of the bipods, line the barrel cradle with felt to protect the finish of the gun. The legs can either be cut in one piece from the same stock as the cradle, or they can be made from sharpened dowels, or from a single sharpened dowel dropping directly below the center of the cradle for use as a monopod.

Whether you build a monopod or bipod depends entirely upon the type of terrain you will be hunting. When hunting rocky terrain the bipod is the better of the two, since it provides lateral support while merely resting on the ground. However, for varmint hunting in fields, pastures, and other soft terrain, the monopod is less bulky to carry and can be shoved down into the ground for superb steadiness. On guns of extremely high recoil—say, anything above the 6mm—stick with the bipod at all time.

To carry the bipod, a small screw eye can be installed near the top on any of these various bipods or monopods, and a lanyard attached so that the bipod can be hung on your belt until needed.

30

Gun Cabinet

Of all the articles of specialized furniture in the home of the sportsman, perhaps none is so prevalent as the gun cabinet. However, have you looked lately at the prices of gun cabinets in the furniture stores—even of the five- or six-gun capacity? You can't get off for less than $100, and more than likely you would have to pay closer to $200 for a cabinet that you can readily build yourself for $20–$30 and a few evenings' work.

This is the most involved project in the book, and has one of the longest bills of materials. Here, the measurements do not follow the usual nominal form of lumber dimensions. Instead, the pieces listed are finished size. In some cases, actual size corresponds to nominal dimensions, and in those instances all you need to worry about is the length of the stock. The other pieces will require gluing and/or rip sawing in order to get the nominal sizes to the proper dimensions.

I recommend you make yourself a kit; that is, before starting the assembly of the cabinet, cut and/or glue each part to size, so that there will be no cutting involved once you begin the assembly. You won't see the cabinet taking form as quickly, but once you begin the actual construction, things will go much faster.

Despite the length of the bill of materials, the construction of the gun cabinet, once the pieces are all cut to size, is quite simple. You will notice that the 16 pieces marked for the legs are optional. I added them to the cabinet shown in the photo because the style matches our own furniture, but there is no reason why you can't simply allow the base cabinet to come all the way to the floor. At least then you won't have to clean under it.

```
                          BILL OF MATERIALS

        2        ¾ × 11 × 52″ pine              cabinet sides
        1        ¾ × 12 × 22″ pine              cabinet top
        1        ¾ × 12¾ × 25″ pine             cabinet bottom
        1        ⅛ × 20¼ × 65″ plywood          cabinet back
        2        ½ × 6½ × 11″ plywood           drawer sides
        2        ½ × 6½ × 22¼″ plywood          drawer front and back
        1        ¾ × 7½ × 23″ pine              drawer false front
        1        ¼ × 11 × 22¼″ plywood          drawer bottom
        2        ¾ × 8 × 12¼″ pine              base cabinet sides
        2        2½ × 51″ frame molding         outer door frame
        2        2½ × 15¼″ frame molding        outer door frame
        2        ¾ × 2 × 45″ pine               inner door frame
        2        ¾ × 2 × 19″ pine               inner door frame
        1        2 × 24″ molding                base molding, front
        2        2 × 12¼″ molding               base molding, sides
       16        2 × 4″ base molding            legs (optional)
        1        ¾ × 3½ × 20¼″ pine             barrel support
        1        ¾ × 10⅞ × 20¼″ pine            butt rack
        1        ¾ × 22¾″ ¼-rnd.                top molding, front
        2        ¾ × 12″ ¼-rnd.                 top molding, sides
        1        ¾ × 12¼ × 24″ plywood          base cabinet bottom
        2        ¾ × ¾ × 49¼″ pine              supports
        4        ¾ × ¾ × 20¼″ pine              supports
        1        49 × 19″ Plexiglas             door glazing
       60        No. 6 × 1¼″ steel wood screws
     1 lb.       4d finishing nails
                 white glue
                 plastic wood
                 stain
                 varnish
        2        cabinet locks
        2        drawer handles
        2        offset hinges
   1 sq. yd.     green felt
```

First, put together the base cabinet. In all joints, use both glue and wood screws. Screw the base cabinet bottom to the base cabinet sides. Attach the bottom piece for the upper cabinet to the upper edges of the base cabinet sides (this piece, obviously, serves double duty). Now turn the base cabinet so that the edges of one entire side of the cube are flush, and put screws through the plywood cabinet

Gun cabinet is a handsome
piece of furniture.

Many sizes of guns are accommodated.

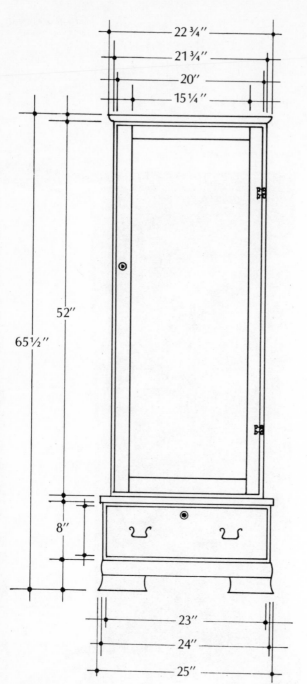

22 ¾″
21 ¾″
20″
15 ¼″

65½″

52″

8″

23″
24″
25″

Cabinet, front view.

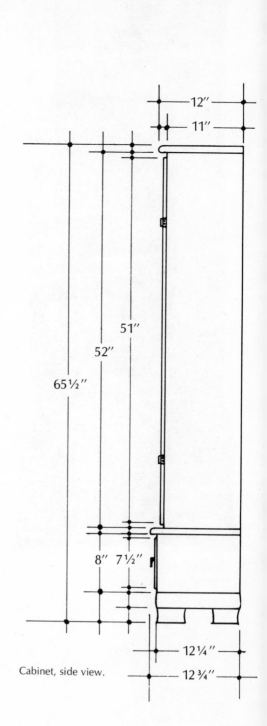

12″
11″

51″

52″

65½″

8″   7½″

Cabinet, side view.

12¼″
12¾″

198

back into the sides, top, and bottom of the base cabinet, making certain that the bottom of the base cabinet is flush with the bottom edge of the cabinet back.

Next, attach the cabinet sides to the cabinet top, positioning the sides against the top so that the top overlaps the sides by ½ inch on each side, and the forward edges of the cabinet sides by 1 inch (see graphed illustration for proper finished dimensions, both side and front view). Now attach the upper cabinet to the cabinet back with glue and wood screws, so that 1⅝ inches of the top of the base cabinet extends outward on either side of the upper cabinet. Reach inside the base cabinet and run three wood screws up through the top of the base cabinet into the bottom edges of the upper cabinet. Now stand the gun cabinet up on its base.

The major part of the construction is now complete. The drawer for the base cabinet is assembled in precisely the same manner as the drawers for the fly-tying desk, Chapter 10. Mortise one of the cabinet locks into the drawer, and attach the lock plate to the top of the base cabinet. All of the cabinet locks come prepackaged, and mortising instructions are on the packages. The only tools you will need are a drill, a mallet, and a small chisel. It looks difficult, but if you take your time, mortising in the lock is much easier and faster than tying a fly or making a fishing plug. Finally, install the drawer handles and the base cabinet is complete. Rub some wax on the drawer to make it slide easily, and install it.

The upper cabinet takes a bit more work. First, take two of the 20¼-inch supports, and attach them to the top of the base cabinet, one flush against the cabinet back, and the front edge of the other flush with the forward edges of the sides of the upper cabinet. These supports are attached with glue and wood screws, and the plywood back of the cabinet is nailed into the rear support with 4d finishing nails. These supports serve not only to strengthen the cabinet, but also provide support for the butt rack, and a lower edge bumper for the door to close against as well.

The butt rack has five ovals cut from it. The holes, for which a graphed pattern is included, measure 2¼ inches wide by 6¼ inches long, and are centered on the panel so that there is 1½ inches of lumber at each end of the panel and 1½ inches in between each of the cutouts. There is a distance of 2¼ inches from the rear of the hole to the rear of the butt rack, and a distance of 2⅜ inches from the front of the hole to the front of the butt rack. Make the cutouts by first increasing the graphed drawing to the correct size and then transferring it to the wood with carbon paper. Drill a hole through the wood inside the drawing, and use a saber saw to cut out the ovals. Now in-

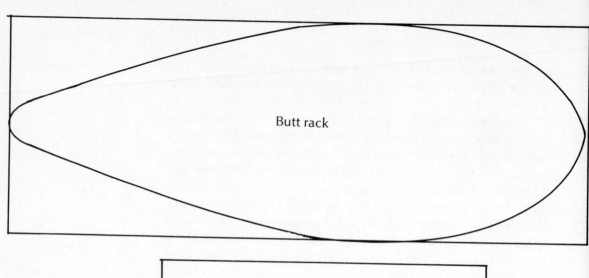

Butt rack

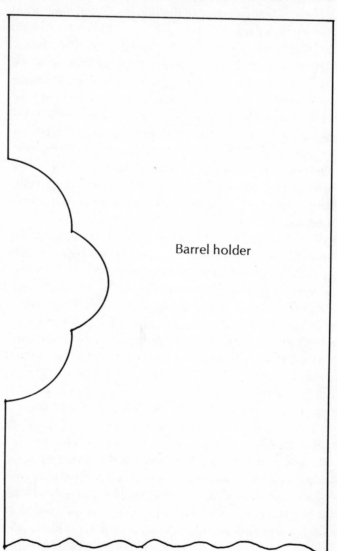

Barrel holder

Pattern for butt rack cutout
and barrel holder cutouts.
Actual size.

stall the butt rack on the bottom supports inside the cabinet with glue and 4d finishing nails. Cut the green felt into strips, and glue the strips around the inside of the cutouts to protect the finish on the gun stocks.

Take the two additional 20¼-inch supports, and affix them to the inside of the top of the cabinet in the same manner in which you affixed the previous two to the bottom. The rear support gives additional strength to the cabinet top/cabinet back bond, while the forward one adds support while providing the upper brace for the door to close against. Next, install the two 49¼-inch supports to the front inside edges of the upper cabinet with glue and wood screws. These supports provide the final braces for the door to close against.

Using the pattern provided, cut out the grooves for the gun barrels in the barrel support. You will notice the rather odd shape of these cutouts. The shape supports both single-barreled weapons, which rest all the way back in the grooves, and double-barreled shotguns as well, which rest in the wider forward groove. Glue this support to the rear of the upper cabinet 30 inches above the butt rack, and drive 4d finishing nails through the cabinet back and sides into the barrel support. Countersink the nail heads, and fill in the holes with plastic wood.

The door frame is double—an outside frame with the vertical members going all the way, and an inside frame with the horizontal members going all the way. The Plexiglas is sandwiched between the frames. The inner frame is ½ inch smaller all around than the outer frame. Build the outer frame first. Then turn it over, molding side down, and lay the Plexiglas on the frame so that there is a ½-inch clearance on all sides. Now carefully drill holes through the Plexiglas, and attach it to the door frame with wood screws. (NO GLUE. Some glues discolor the Plexiglas and make it brittle.) Then position the inner frame and screw the sandwich together. I use Plexiglas rather than regular glass for two reasons: the material can be drilled and screwed, eliminating the problems of glazing with special moldings, clips, and putty; and, it seems ridiculous to me to put a lock on the door of a gun cabinet and then make that door out of a material that can be shattered as easily as glass.

Finally, mortise the second cabinet lock into the door frame, install the lock plate to the side of the upper cabinet, and mount the cabinet door onto the cabinet with the two offset hinges. The thickness of the door requires the use of the offset rather than the standard butt hinges. At this point the cabinet is built and ready to use, except for the finishing touches. The base molding is cut at a 45-degree angle and nailed and glued around the base cabinet, to provide a finish to the bottom of the cabinet. The quarter-round molding is attached to the edges of the cabinet top, to finish that point. In all instances, the molding is attached with glue and 4d finishing nails, the heads of which are countersunk and filled with plastic wood.

The optional legs are made by cutting the molding at a 45-degree angle and gluing and nailing 4-inch sections together to form a cube. Do this four times, and you have four sturdy but attractive legs. Glue them to the bottom, and set the cabinet on them. There is no need to clamp them, since the weight of the cabinet will keep them in place until the glue dries. Install a strip of felt along the barrel holder, and the cabinet is ready to stain and varnish. And when the finish is dry, put your guns in the upper cabinet, shells and cleaning equipment (along with calls, licenses, and other small paraphernalia) in the drawer, lock them up, and you have a beautiful and safe place to store your hunting equipment.

IV

TIPS
AND TRICKS

31
Tips and
Tricks

If you have carried through the 28 projects in this book, you probably are tired of building things. But you have 28 new accessories for hunting, fishing, and your home, at a total cost of probably less than $100. That is, on the average, less than $3 a project. When you figure that that includes a fishing rod rack, a gun cabinet, a wooden tackle box, and a custom-fitted shotgun case, among other things, that is quite a bit of savings.

But many other accessories which the sportsman can make could not be classed as projects. Some utilize scraps from other projects, or bits and pieces that are commonly found around the house. Most of them won't cost you a cent, and the few that do cost you pennies rather than dollars.

MASON JAR BAIT CONTAINER:

An ordinary Ball mason jar, the type that is used for canning, makes a handy container for live bait such as frogs, grasshoppers, and the like. Discard the ball cap with the rubber seal, but keep the screw-on retaining ring. Now cut a piece of window screen into a circle and fit it into the retaining ring. Put the bait in the jar, and screw the ring back on. The screen allows the bait to breathe, so it lives a lot longer.

SAWDUST BAIT PRESERVATIVE:

If you use grass shrimp as bait, and freeze them, they will retain their shape and stay on the hook better if they are frozen in sawdust rather than simply lumped together. Take some of the sawdust from one of your projects. Fill a freezer container half full of shrimp, and add sawdust to bring the amount of material up to ¾ of the container. Put the lid on and shake well, add another handful of sawdust and shake again. This distributes the bait and the sawdust evenly throughout the container. Now stick it in the freezer until you are ready to use it. The sawdust soaks up some of the juices of the shrimp, and can be used as an effective chum or scent trail by throwing a few pinches overboard at a time.

FLY LINE STORAGE REEL:

Oatmeal boxes make handy storage reels to prevent the tight curls that get in fly lines, if they are left on the fly reel too long. Oatmeal comes in 1-pound, and 2-pound 10-ounce round boxes. Take one of the 1-pound boxes, and wind the fly line in loose coils around it. Now set this one down inside the larger oatmeal box, put the lid back on, and label the top. The outer box prevents anything from rubbing against and abrading the line while it is being stored.

SPOOL BOBBER:

In our plastic age, even thread spools are being made of foam plastic instead of wood. These, however, can be turned into effective bobbers for spin fishermen. Put a small snap swivel on the end of your line, and thread it and the line through the hole in the center of the spool. Now hook the snap swivel onto a snelled hook, slide the spool up your line to the point you want it, and wedge a small stick or ¼-inch dowel into the hole, pinning the line to the side.

SMALL HACKSAW:

There are many times when a small hacksaw would be of use to the sportsman. One can be made by taking a regular hacksaw blade and breaking it in half. Wrap the broken end with several turns of electrical or adhesive tape. That makes one end rounded, and one end covered, so it can easily be carried in a pocket of your hunting coat. Wrap the other half in the same way, and tuck it in your tackle box.

WHISTLE:

Ever need to communicate with a hunting buddy who was out of sight, but not want to run through the woods shouting like a maniac? Carry a spent cartridge case in your pocket, and blow across the top of the case mouth. It makes a low pitched whistle which is easily heard for almost a mile.

CASE TRIMMER DIE:

If you have a cartridge case trimmer that uses centering dies through which the cartridge neck protrudes rather than pilots, you can make extra dies very easily. Drill a hole in a block of wood the size of the case neck, and force the neck of the case down into it. It should be a tight fit. Now cut the bottom out of one of the little aluminum cans that 35mm film comes in, and set it over the case so that the can is exactly centered. Use electrical tape to tape the can in place. Now melt bar solder (not the kind with flux added) in a small pot, either with a torch or over the stove burner, and fill the film can. Since the solder is not fluxed, it will not stick to the case when it hardens. Drive the case out, file away any places where the solder escaped around the bottom of the can, and your case trimmer die is ready to use.

WRAP-AROUND SINKERS:

Ever needed to sink a fly, or some bait, just a little, and not had a sinker light enough? Take an empty toothpaste tube and split it along one side, and across the top and bottom. Wash all traces of tooth-paste off the metal. Now cut the tube into strips ¼ inch wide. Place them in a plastic pill bottle. They can be wrapped around the line as is, and they are workable enough to break in half with the fingers if even less weight is needed.

FIX YOUR BIRD'S NESTS:

There has never been a fisherman who has not suffered a backlash, or bird's nest, with his fishing reel. To attempt to get two or more fingers into the reel spool and pull out a loop at a time is frustrating to say the least. Carry a simple crochet hook in your tackle box. You'll be surprised how rapidly you can free a line-jammed reel with the little hooked tool.

HOOK DISGORGER:

A hook disgorger is designed to remove the hook from a fish's mouth without injuring the fish, even if it is very deeply hooked. But even the small ends of the commercial disgorgers are large enough to severely injure a small fish when they are shoved down its throat. If you purchased the set of cheap screwdrivers, you have several that you don't normally use. Take one with a medium-sized blade, and, with a three-cornered file, file a "V"-shaped notch into the blade end. Round any sharp edges with emery paper. Slide the notch down the line, into the fish's mouth until it contacts the hook, and push, giving a quarter turn to the handle. Draw the disgorger and the hook back out, keeping tension on the line to keep the hook snugged up against the disgorger. Different sizes can easily be made for different sized fish, and the cheap screwdrivers that are used for them cost less than a commercial disgorger.

SINKER MOLD:

Unless you are a shape traditionalist, sinker molds can be made quite easily. Drill holes of the size you need in a scrap of 2×4, pour in the melted lead, and before it has hardened, set a small screw eye in the top. After the sinkers have thoroughly cooled, you should be able to turn the block over, pick it up by one end, smack the other end against the edge of the workbench, and have the sinkers fall out. If they won't, the "mold" is cheap enough that you can split it along the line of the holes and then make another when you need more. If you want to make sliding sinkers, take a finishing nail, dip it in powdered graphite, and drive it into the center of the hole in the mold, very lightly. After the lead has hardened, the head of the nail can be grasped with a pair of pliers and twisted out, leaving a small hole through the center of the sinker for the line to slide through.

PANFISH FLOAT:

Need a light float for panfish? A plastic soda straw makes a fine substitute for a porcupine quill. Twist a loop of copper wire tightly around the middle, squeeze the ends shut and seal them together so they won't fill with water by melting them slightly with your cigarette lighter.

INSTAMATIC PROTECTION:

Although the Instamatic cameras are very durable snapshot cameras to take into the field, a brush against an oarlock or a rock or thorn can destroy the plastic lens. No lens caps are available for them as they are for more expensive cameras, but one can easily be made from the cap of a plastic pill bottle. Look around until you find one which fits tightly enough so that it won't fall off. The small lip on the cap makes it easy to remove when you want to take a picture.

SHIRT-TAIL LURE:

Caught without bait, and the stripers or blues are breaking? Tear a strip off your shirt-tail, or use a piece of rag that you have used to wipe out the boat, and weave the hook and line through it. I don't know what the fish think it is—maybe an eel—but it works. The rag from the boat works even better, probably because it has picked up fish slime which gives off a bait odor in the water.

MINNOW BUCKET:

Take a 2-pound coffee can and punch it full of holes. Make sure that they are punched from the inside out, so that there will be no jagged edges inside to injure the minnows. Now fill a 3-pound coffee can with water, put the perforated can inside it, and place the minnows in the inner can. When you need a bait, lift up the inner can. The water will drain out of the holes, and you can easily select—and pick up—the minnow of your choice. If you have the plastic resealable lid for the 1-pound can, you can attach a line to that can, snap the lid on, and hang it overboard. It will sink, but the lid will keep the minnows in, and the circulating water will keep them alive much longer.

FLY DRIER:

If a fly is allowed to dry of its own accord, often the feathers will mat together, and it will have to be steamed in order to restore it to shape. This is a lot of trouble and can easily be avoided. Take all of the flies that are wet or have dried matted together, and drop them in a bucket of water for ten minutes. Hook the hose of the vacuum cleaner up to the blower end, and put the wet flies in a pouch made of window screen. Wire this pouch onto the other end of the hose. The hot air blowing over the flies will dry them in about ten minutes, and will keep them dancing around in the screen pouch so they will not mat together.

PAPER CASE REJUVENATOR:

If you are still shooting paper shotshells (as I am) you probably have several that are very difficult to reload because the mouths are severely frayed. If there has been no head separation, these cases can easily be reclaimed. Melt some paraffin in a double boiler (never melt paraffin directly over a burner unless you want one hell of a fire; if you don't have a double boiler, put the paraffin in a coffee can, and set the can into a Dutch oven or large frying pan filled with water over the stove). Now dip about 1 inch of the case into the paraffin for about two minutes, so that it gets thoroughly saturated. Hold it upside down above the can so that any excess paraffin can drip off. Let the cases dry overnight, and then resize them. They'll be just like new. The die will have to be cleaned after each box of shells, but saving those extra cases is more than worth the extra trouble.

The Versatile
Plastic Jug

I have saved the most versatile bit of material for last: the plastic jug. This is a potential accessory that is free, and almost always discarded. Many things come in plastic jugs—bleach, fabric softener, various cleaners, floor wax and so on—and they range in size from quart to gallon. The gallon size is the most versatile of them all.

JUG FISHING:

This is an old time sport, and a very relaxing way to catch a mess of delicious, fat catfish for dinner. Tie a 4-foot length of line to the handle of a gallon jug, bait it with a 2/0 hook and a chunk of liver. Heave several of them overboard, sit back, open up a good book, and drift with the current. Glance at the jugs from time to time. When a big cat grabs the bait and the jug goes bobbing off quickly down the current there'll be plenty of action. When two or four head off in opposite directions at the same time you'll know how exciting this "lazy" fishing can really be.

JUG FLOAT:

Jugs in the half-gallon or gallon size make excellent floats for trotlines, whether used for fishing or crabbing. Use the white bleach jugs. They are easy to locate, and they keep other boaters from running across your line.

JUG ANCHORS:

Here we go in exactly the opposite direction. Just mix up some Portland cement or ready-mixed concrete and fill a gallon jug with it. The handle provides the place to tie your line. Although this anchor won't hold a large boat, or a medium sized boat in a heavy wind, it is an excellent general-purpose anchor. It won't get caught in snags on the bottom, and the plastic "coating" makes it very easy to wash the mud off, keeping the inside of your boat a lot cleaner.

BOAT SCOOP:

Cut the bottom out of a gallon plastic jug, and use it to bail out the boat. The handle of the jug makes a much better scoop handle than I have ever found on commercial scoops, and the extreme flexibility of the plastic lets the scoop conform to most boat interiors.

FOR BOW FISHERMEN:

Bow reels are nice, and all that, but I gave up on them years ago because of their disconcerting habit of dumping coils of line over the arrow, causing a monster of a snarl, whenever I was going to shoot at a fish. Tie a 20-foot length of line onto your arrow, and tie the other end to a half-gallon plastic jug. Coil the line neatly on the boat seat. It will follow the arrow quite easily, and most fish are not shot at distances over 20 feet anyway. If you strike the fish, toss the jug overboard and follow it until the fish weakens, then haul him aboard.

SHOT CONTAINER:

Half-gallon plastic jugs make much better shot containers than the cloth bags that the lead shot comes in. They are easy to label with a Magic Marker, and the handles make it much, much simpler to pour the shot into the measure without having a couple of ounces escape and wind up all over the floor.

BOAT FENDERS:

Fill quart plastic jugs with water and tie them so they hang just over the edge of the boat. The water in the jugs provides a hydraulic cushioning to protect the boat from rubbing or bumping against other boats, piers or pilings.

APPENDIX

Where to Find it

Brookstone Company 12 Brookstone Building Peterborough, New Hampshire 03458	Special tools and materials

Fenwick/Sevenstrand
   Tackle Manufacturing
14799 Chestnut Street
Westminster, California
          92683
	Various types of wire

Finnysports
2910 Glanzman Road
Toledo, Ohio
          43614
	Plug hardware, special woods
	   in hard to find sizes

Fly Fisherman's Bookcase Route 9A Croton-on-Hudson, New York 10520	Fly-tying materials

Herter's, Inc.
Route 2
Mitchell, South Dakota
          57301
	Plug hardware, wire, tools,
	   fly-tying materials

E. Hille
815 Railway Street
P. O. Box 269
Williamsport, Pennsylvania
          17701
	Plug hardware, wooden plug
	   bodies, tools

Midland Tackle Company
66 Route 17
Sloatsburg, New York
10974

Net twine and tools

Netcraft Company
3101 Sylvania Avenue
Toledo, Ohio
43613

Plug hardware, net twine and
materials, tools, wire

Woodcraft Supply Corporation
313 Montvale Avenue
Woburn, Massachusetts
01801

Fine woodworking tools, hobby
woods

INDEX

accessories for hunters and fishermen,
 necessity and cost of, 3–4
acrylic artists' colors, 168, 171
aerosol spray paint, 81
alligator clips, 24–28

balsa wood, 78
bending jig, 114–116
birds' nests in line, coping with, 207
bits, drill, 8
Black Ghost flies, 29
"block" (working decoy), 163
boat box for tackle, 52–54
boat fenders, plastic jugs for, 212
boat scoop, plastic jug, 211
bobbers, thread spools for, 206
bow reels, plastic jugs for, 211
brace and bit, 8, 10
brass fittings, 140
 for tackle box, 46, 50–51
 for squirrel call, 180, 182
 for crow call, 189
brass screws, 16, 59, 167
butt joints, 149

camera case, fisherman's, 19–22
cameras, instamatic, protection for, 208–209

cardboard, corrugated, for dove decoys, 173, 176
cedar wood for plug bodies, 78
chalk, 187
chisels, wood, 9–10, 163, 180, 182, 199
circular saw, 11, 45
clamps, 8, 57–58, 165
contour gauge, 79
coping saw, 6, 58, 166, 184, 186
corks, cutting, for plugs, 97–99
costs of commercially made sports equipment, 3, 20, 44, 55, 76, 129, 133, 136, 151, 156, 162, 188, 195
costs of materials for homemade projects, 4, 20, 30, 41, 55, 61, 73, 78, 93, 100, 101, 102, 110, 126, 129, 133, 137, 144, 151, 153, 156, 180, 195
costs of tools, 6, 7, 8, 9, 11, 12
countersink, 11, 69, 201
crows, hunting, 172, 188
cup hooks, 69–70

decorative decoys, 170–171
decoys, 5
 ducks, 162
 silhouette dove, 172
dies for case trimmers, 207

dowel sizes and cartridge sizes
    compared, 130–131
dowels, 191
    using, for plug bodies, 79, 81–82
drawers, building, 63, 67–69,
    112–113, 196
drills, hand, 8, 184
drills, power, 12–14, 149, 158
Duco cement, 60, 89

eel fly, 35–37
enamel, 85, 150–151
epoxy cement, 59, 191
epoxy paint, 54, 139, 150
epoxy spray enamels, 85
eyes, glass, for decoys, 170–171

field dressing of game, 142
files, 184, 186, 188
film cans, 31, 33, 70, 71, 74
fishing equipment, handmade, 4,
    19, 23, 29, 35, 38, 41, 42, 52,
    55, 63, 72, 76, 92, 95, 100,
    117
fly drier, 209
fly–drying rack, 8
fly line, storing safely, 206
fly tying, 5, 23, 28, 29, 34, 35–37,
    38–40, 63
foam rubber, 20, 21–22

galvanized finishing nails, 52
game carrier, 5, 142
gauge for use in net weaving, 102,
    103, 106
Ginger Quill fly, 28
glue, 16, 20, 22, 57–58, 73, 74,
    97, 114, 140
gun cabinet, 5, 7, 8, 195
gun case, 5, 136

hacksaw, 96, 97
    making a small, 206
hammers, 7
    see also mallets

handloading, 5
hand tools, 6–11
hasp and padlock, 54
hatch fly patterns, 29
handloading, 125, 151
hardwood, necessity of, in turkey
    call, 183–184
Heddon Company, 76
Herters Company, 101
Hester's Finnysports, 76
hobby wood stores, 184
hook attachments for wooden plus,
    89–90
hook disgorger, 207–208
hooks, 36
hunting equipment and acces-
    sories, handmade, 125, 136,
    142, 147, 152, 155, 162, 172,
    179, 183, 188, 190, 195

jag anchors, 211
Jock Scott flies, 29
jug fishing, 210
jug floats, 210–211

keels, decoy, placing and mount-
    ing, 167
knife, pocket, 8

live cars, 100
lumber, see plywood; wood
lure trays, constructing,
    47–50

mallets, 163, 180, 182, 199
March Browns, 75
mason jars for live bait, 205
Masonite, 128, 149–150
materials of limited use, 6
measure stand/die rack,
    133–135
midge vise, 5, 14, 16,
    23–28, 34
minnow bucket, coffee cans for,
    209

miter joints, 43, 54
monopods, 191, 194

nail set, 11, 69, 201
nails, 15–16, 24
Netcraft Company, 76, 101, 108, 109
Netcraft Wheel, 102
nets, weaving, 61–62, 100–109
netting knots, 104, 106
nonessential accessories for sportsmen, 4
nylon twine, bonded, 101, 102

paint as wood finish, 139
painting decoys, 167–170
painting plug bodies, 81, 95
panfish float, 208
paper shell rejuvenator, 210
papier-mâché for dove decoys, 177–178
perfection loops, 104, 106
pill vials, 32
planes, 10
plastic jugs, multiple uses of, 210–212
plastic wood, see wood fillers
plastic worms, 41
plexiglass, 201
pliers, 8
plugs, wooden, 76–91
plywood, 14, 15, 52, 73, 74, 112–113, 128, 133, 135, 139, 144, 153, 172, 191, 199
popping bugs, cork-bodied, 95
power saws, 11–12
precision loads, 132

rasps, wood, 59–60, 164–165
reloading block, no-danger, 129–133
reloading dies, 135
reels, displaying, 122
ring-barb siding nails, 128
rings, live bag, 108

rope clamps, 58
rug protectors, 121

saber saw, 11, 45
salmon eggs, 38
sandpapering, 10, 46, 60, 69, 74, 97, 114, 165, 170, 186
sawdust for preserving frozen bait, 205–206
saws, 6, 45, 97
    see also power saws
scale, fisherman's, 93
screening, attaching, 144–145
screw starters, 11, 90
screwdrivers, 7–8
screws, 16
sheet bend knot, 104, 106
shell carrier, 5
shirt-tail lures, 209
shot container, plastic jug for, 211
shotgun shells, 130
shotshell sizes, 148–149
shuttles for net weaving, 101, 102
sinker molds, 208
sinkers, improvised wrap-around, 207
slots for dividers in wood trays, cutting, 48–49
sources for materials, 213–214
spinning box, 43–51
square, carpenter's, 8–9, 128
squirrel call, 5, 9
squirrels, hunting, 179, 182
stain, see wood finishes
staple guns, 144
Surform tool, 10–11, 59

tacklebox, wooden, 8, 41–54
    metal, 20–21
thread clip, 70, 74
through-wire construction of plugs, 78, 87–89
tools, hand, 24
trimming shotshells for uniformity in reloading, 155, 160
tripods, 191

trolling line, color-coded, 92
trout net, wooden-frame, 55–62
turkeys, hunting, 183, 187

varnishing wood, 47, 61, 74, 114,
    139, 180
vinyl wallpaper, 138–139
vises, 23

wet flies, 37–40
whistles, improvised, 206–207

wiggle plates, 78, 90
wire former, commercial, 114
wood, 14–15
wood fillers, 46, 69, 73, 201
wood finishes, 46, 61, 114,
    137–138, 139, 180

X-Acto knives, 79, 170

Zar acrylic finish, 47, 61, 69